THE
UNEXPECTED
JOURNEY

EMBRACING THE BEAUTY OF DISABILITY

JULIE FISHER

First published by Ultimate World Publishing 2019
Copyright © 2019 Julie Fisher

ISBN

Paperback - 978-1-925884-41-8
Ebook - 978-1-925884-42-5

Julie Fisher has asserted her right under the Copyright, Designs and Patents Act 1988 to be identified as the author of this work. The information in this book is based on the author's experiences and opinions. The publisher specifically disclaims responsibility for any adverse consequences, which may result from use of the information contained herein. Permission to use information has been sought by the author. Any breaches will be rectified in further editions of the book.

All rights reserved. No part of this publication may be reproduced, stored in or introduced into a retrieval system, or transmitted in any form, or by any means (electronic, mechanical, photocopying, recording or otherwise) without the prior written permission of the author. Any person who does any unauthorised act in relation to this publication may be liable to criminal prosecution and civil claims for damages. Enquiries should be made through the publisher.

Cover design: Ultimate World Publishing
Layout and typesetting: Ultimate World Publishing
Editor: Hayley Ward

Ultimate World Publishing
Diamond Creek,
Victoria Australia 3089
www.writeabook.com.au

TESTIMONIALS

The overwhelming message for me from The Unexpected Journey is to embrace and educate, of which Julie has done, and continues to do, fiercely and lovingly. More importantly is the love and joy that Darcy brings and the education that he has provided simply by being himself — to his family, his village and beyond.

Molly Morelli

I first met Darcy Fisher and his family when Darcy was three. I still vividly recall Darcy visiting our school in a stroller. Darcy was a three-year-old boy who could not walk, could not talk and required a PEG to assist him with feeding. Despite these challenges, Darcy and his family could not have been more positive. It was clear from the combination of laughter and tears that this boy was much loved and fun to be around.

Since that time, I have been privileged to watch Darcy grow into an independent young man respected by his peers and teachers. Darcy has always maintained his cheeky grin and sense of adventure as he continues to make achievements that defy expectations. I do believe part of Darcy's success could be attributed to his family's drive to include him in their everyday lives and as an active member of their community.

Darcy was an honorary member of his brother's football team and I have great memories of him showing me the premiership medallion he was awarded when the team won their grand final.

I was honoured to attend Darcy's graduation at Langwarrin Park Primary School (LPPS) last year.

Darcy attended LPPS one day a week for his primary education. This was the school his two older brothers attended. He was clearly a popular member of the class.

I look forward to watching Darcy grow and develop in his secondary years at Frankston Special Developmental School.

Scott Tucker
Principal
Frankston SDS & Blackwood SSOEC

It has been my pleasure to know Julie and her family for over 20 years. At the heart of everything that Julie does is love for family. This has only grown since the arrival of Darcy. Julie not only ensures that his therapy and educational needs are met, but also that his social and emotional needs are too. Darcy is given every opportunity to experience life and be successful. While it has not been an easy road, Julie is determined to give every opportunity to her family. Such a close family that sees the joy in disability! How Lucky Darcy is to be a part of the Fisher family!

Erin Alford
Teacher
Frankston Special Developmental School

Darcy has been surrounded by so much love and support his whole life and it has been an honour to be part of his and his family's journey. He has grown so much and is always working so hard to increase his independence. I am so excited to read this book. Well done Julie!

Kate Wormell
Occupational Therapist
Sprout Paediatric Therapy Services

I have known the Fisher Family since before they were a family – I've known Julie and Mick for roughly 32 years!

Even before they became a family unit Julie and Mick had a very strong bond and have always supported each other with an unwavering love. Their bond increased as each child was born.

They have instilled their values and love onto each child, which has made the transition into a family of a Down Syndrome child and they've taken it in their stride as they have done with every other major or minor life event that has come their way. Julie and Mick haven't wondered 'Why Me?' They have only ever wondered 'Why Not Me?'!

The Fisher family have embraced having a child with Down Syndrome whole-heartedly and joyfully, focusing on the positives that outweigh any negatives; feeling blessed with the gift they have received in the form of a Down Syndrome child named Darcy.

Julie Lowe

> **"When life gives you a hundred reasons to cry, show life you have a thousand reasons to smile."**
>
> (Author unknown)

This is my favourite quote, and one that most definitely applies to Julie Fisher, who saw a future for Darcy before he was even born; she saw light and opportunity, where others saw darkness, obstacles and ignorance. Having a child with a disability changes you in ways you never thought possible; it makes you laugh until you wet yourself, it makes you so proud you feel like your heart could burst, it makes you cry until there are no tears left; ultimately it makes you into a stronger person that you never knew existed until now and an advocate for your child with the fighting spirit of a world champion.

Julie finds a thousand reasons to smile each and every day, through her love for her hubby and the unconditional love she has for all her boys.

This book is a gift; read it, treasure it and most of all learn that there is always a reason to smile!

Tina Naughton

Special parents are given special children. Already having two beautiful boys, Julie and Mick always knew Darcy would have Down Syndrome and never once did they shy away from any responsibility that went along with that. Darcy, with his big personality, brings happiness to many people who have been involved in his life and is truly a beautiful person. I get excited when I talk about the Fisher family as they are great people, lifetime friends and great ambassadors for Down Syndrome.

Julie is a truly remarkable person. Joolz is my best friend from my school days and I'm so happy to have known her for over 35 years.

Julie has always been a happy and placid person; always smiling, she gives 100% to everything she's involved in. When Joolz said she was going to put pen to paper and share this journey I was so excited for her, I know it'll be a fantastic read about their journey, the highs and lows, and the great family bond they share between the five of them. Awesome work Julie Fisher and so proud of you xx

Liz Patane

CONTENTS

Testimonials 3
Dedication... 11
Thank You... 13
Welcome To Holland 15
Introduction 17
CHAPTER 1: Something Is Different 21
CHAPTER 2: Verdict 31
CHAPTER 3: Cycle Of Grief 41
CHAPTER 4: Demystifying Down Syndrome 49
CHAPTER 5: Getting Ready For The Baby 57
CHAPTER 6: He's Here 65
CHAPTER 7: Embracing Uncertainty 75
CHAPTER 8: Beyond Complications 83
CHAPTER 9: Part Of The Tribe 97
CHAPTER 10: New Normal 105
CHAPTER 11: Life 2.0 121
CHAPTER 12: Acceptance/Inclusion 137
About The Author 141
Links for support groups, therapy services and groups......... 144
The Unexpected Journey.. 145

DEDICATION

I would like to dedicate my book to my family - my husband Mick, my sons Caleb, Blake and Darcy and my stepdaughter Bree (our gypsy). Through good times and bad, they guide and teach me every day and have made me who I am. Their support through this journey has been amazing and has inspired me to keep going and follow my dream. And here is my dream for everyone to enjoy.

THANK YOU

Thank you also to my beautiful band of friends who have supported me and lifted me when I've doubted myself. My special friends, you all know who you are, have most certainly helped me stay on track and keep focused on my goal. Without all of you, I don't think I would be where I am today.

Julie and Liz, my longest friends. Your support and encouragement has been second to none and you've both definitely lifted me when I needed it.

Joel Comelli, thank you for providing me with a most valuable source to help finish my book and for your help setting up my website.

Tracey McCartney, my wonderful friend, thank you for taking the cover photo for my book. It took a few attempts, but you managed to capture the perfect photo.

WELCOME TO HOLLAND

WRITTEN BY EMILY PERL KINGSLEY

I am often asked to describe the experience of raising a child with a disability – to try to help people who have not shared that unique experience to understand it, to imagine how it would feel. It's like this...

When you're going to have a baby, it's like planning a fabulous vacation trip – to Italy. You buy a bunch of guidebooks and make your wonderful plans. The Coliseum. The Michelangelo David. The gondolas in Venice. You learn some handy phrases in Italian. It's all very exciting.

After months of eager anticipation, the day finally arrives. You pack your bags and off you go. Several hours later, the plane lands. The stewardess comes in and says, "Welcome to Holland".

"Holland?!?" you say. "What do you mean Holland?? I signed up for Italy! I'm supposed to be in Italy. All my life I've dreamed of going to Italy."

The Unexpected Journey

But there's been a change in the flight plan. They've landed in Holland and there you must stay.

The important thing is that they haven't taken you to a horrible, disgusting, filthy place, full of pestilence, famine and disease. It's just a different place.

So, you must go out and buy new guidebooks. And you must learn a whole new language. And you will meet a whole new group of people you would never have met.

It's just a different place. It's slower-paced than Italy, less flashy than Italy. But after you've been there for a while and you catch your breath, you look around…and you begin to notice that Holland has windmills…and Holland has tulips. Holland even has Rembrandts.

But everyone you know is busy coming and going from Italy…and they're all bragging about what a wonderful time they had there. And for the rest of your life, you will say "Yes, that's where I was supposed to go. That's what I had planned."

And the pain of that will never, ever, ever, ever go away…because the loss of that dream is a very, very significant loss.

But…if you spend your life mourning the fact that you didn't get to Italy, you may never be free to enjoy the very special, the very lovely things…about Holland.

This is a poem parents receive from Down Syndrome Victoria when they contact them after diagnosis. It is very true, and I am so happy I ended up in Holland.

INTRODUCTION

The dream to write a book has been with me since I was a teenager. I used to love it when given the task of writing a long essay in high school and turning an idea into a story.

My dream started to become something that would turn into reality when I attended the Ultimate 48 Hour Author Seminar in Mornington in May 2018. It was an emotional day for me as I realised the dream was a real burn inside me bursting to get out.

My meeting with Natasa Denman after the seminar was like something out of a book. When she said they would love to help me realise my dream, I was elated. I signed up on the spot and immediately started planning my book.

Initially, I had always wanted to write about something else in my life, but when Natasa asked me what my book would be about, I told her I would like to share the story of our journey with our son Darcy. It just came out and so I thought, well that is what I need to write about.

The Unexpected Journey

Almost 12 months later I found myself at the Ultimate 48 Hour Author Retreat along with 16 other budding authors. Fear, excitement, happiness, nervousness all bundled into one when we all entered the room.

Standing up to tell everyone what my book was about and revealing the cover was very emotional for me, but the response from everyone just reinstated the fact that I was doing the right thing.

With the support of everyone at the retreat and my mentors Stuart and Natasa Denman and Vivienne, as well as my amazing friends and the best family a girl could ask for, I have realised my dream.

I hope you enjoy the journey as much as we have so far. There are emotional times, scary times, sad times but most of all happy and amazing moments in the world of disability we have become a part of.

I thank my little man for choosing us to look after him and try and make the best life possible for him.

"There is no greater disability in society, than the inability to see a person as more."

Robert M Hensel

CHAPTER 1

SOMETHING IS DIFFERENT

I had always dreamed of being married with three or four kids, so when Mick proposed to me very early in our relationship, I was very excited, and of course I said yes. I couldn't wait to get married. We weren't living together, and we'd only been seeing each other for a short time, but we knew it was right, and it was very exciting. However, 11 years went past before we actually got married, and what a great day that was.

Because it was so long from engagement to marriage, we were in a bit of a hurry to start our family, so one month later we became pregnant with our first son, Caleb. Pregnancy was a dream for me. I loved it. I loved watching my belly grow, and welcoming Caleb into the world was one of the best moments in my life. He was such a gorgeous little baby. Three years later we got pregnant with Blake, and again, it was one of the best feelings in the world, bringing that little boy into the world. Gorgeous little boys, perfectly beautiful and healthy. There were a few ups and downs, as with any children, and a couple of minor medical issues along the way early in their lives, but they were perfect in every way, just beautiful.

So, life went on busily running a household and working full-time. The boys were both in primary school and played football and basketball. Before we knew it, five years had passed, and my biological clock started ticking. I always wanted to have that third baby to complete our family. I was 36 and Mick was 42, so we thought we were probably starting to get a bit old to have another child, but that burn was still there for me. It was a joint decision. I didn't really feel complete without another child. I don't know why, I just always wanted to have three kids.

Weeks had passed since that conversation and we hadn't changed anything we were doing, but I was late. We thought I was pregnant, and we were pretty excited. I was over the moon and felt like I was floating. Almost two weeks later, and thinking I was pregnant…. NO! False alarm. I did so many tests in between and even though they were all negative, I still thought I was pregnant. It was very early stages and the pregnancy kits don't always pick it up when it's that early. I was driving everybody mad! The sorrow I felt when we found out I wasn't pregnant was huge. I was so sure.

After the false alarm and realising how upset we were that there was no pregnancy cemented the fact that we really did want to have another child. We were both quite excited at the thought of extending our family and bringing another little one into the world. It didn't take long…two months later I was pregnant again. Right from the start I loved being pregnant. I'd always loved the feeling of that little person growing inside. I was glowing.

Something Is Different

I did pregnancy very well all three times, and even though I felt amazing, I felt that this pregnancy was a little different from the others. I didn't know why.

My first thoughts were that perhaps it was a girl this time. I thought that would be perfect, to have a little girl with two little boys. Everybody wants one of each or two of each…you know, pigeon pair. I didn't let it stay in my thoughts for too long. I didn't let it rule me, I just thought "Oh, well, it's probably a girl this time, because it's a bit different." Everything else felt right, it just wasn't the same as the boys, but I loved being pregnant again. I loved watching my tummy grow and watching the movement as the baby got bigger. It's the best feeling in the world. I think women are very lucky to be able to bring life into the world and watch them grow. It's an amazing miracle, and the feeling for me was fantastic.

So, we are 10 weeks into the pregnancy and the time came for mandatory blood tests and an ultrasound. I only had an ultrasound with the other boys, but they told me this was a new screening to put you into a high or low-risk category. I was very busy and couldn't get my appointments at the same time. So, I had my blood tests and then about two weeks later I had the ultrasound. I didn't really think anything of it.

I just went to a local Gribbles Pathology. Because of where I was working and the hours I was working, I couldn't get into the obstetrician that I'd used for the other two boys. The stenographer was a nice man, and very thorough. The only thing that worried me was that he kept measuring the thickness of the neck on the baby on the back of the head. I knew from my friend Tina that was a sign they looked for with Down Syndrome. It's to do with the shape of the head which makes the neck thickness bigger. Tina has a beautiful daughter Amy who happens to have Down Syndrome and I'd become quite close with them.

I asked him why he kept measuring the neck thickness and he told me he was being thorough and making sure he had the correct measurements. I lay there wondering why. He measured the thickness about four or five times, so I asked him again. He told me again he wanted to make sure his measurements were right. I was getting concerned and asked him if he thought the baby had Down Syndrome. He told me no, although he couldn't quite say. He said he was no expert but all the organs in the baby looked great so he would be surprised if the baby had Down Syndrome.

Eventually, he explained that if the measurements are over 3mm they usually put you in the high-risk category. He said the measurements of my baby's neck were just under that - 2.8 - 2.9 - and that's why he kept checking, to make sure it wasn't 3mm or over. It sparked a bit of worry in my mind and I started to think, "Oh no, well what if something else is wrong? What if there's something else wrong internally? Don't kids with Down Syndrome have lots of internal problems? Don't they have lots of doctor's visits and operations?" That was my perception of children with Down Syndrome. I thought they were constantly in hospital, constantly having operation after operation.

I thought to myself, "Oh, well what if the baby does have Down Syndrome? What's going to happen?" And this was all while I was laying on the bed having the ultrasound, so I asked him what he thought I should do. I told him if the baby has Down Syndrome, I want to know. He told me I should probably get a second opinion, but they'd probably tell me the same thing, that they wouldn't know and wouldn't be able to tell me officially because they can't with just the ultrasound. I would have to have further testing to be 100%.

Something Is Different

So, I left his office, and I went home and talked to Mick and the boys about it. I told them I thought the baby had Down Syndrome. I told them why and what the stenographer had said. I remember us thinking, the pregnancy's just like the other boys, it's all going well and the baby's growing. All sorts of things were going through our heads. I told Mick I just had a feeling (especially after the ultrasound) that the baby had Down Syndrome. We talked about it and decided that we would get the extra testing done so we could be sure. I wanted to be able to tell everyone so that we could prepare.

Tina and I had become friends because her eldest daughter and Caleb were at school together. I had spoken to her about her daughter Amy, who has Down Syndrome, and asked her about when she was born. She told me how upsetting it was to be told the news after the birth. It's an unknown world and nobody knows what to expect. That little perfect bubble that we all want for our children is taken away so dramatically straight after giving birth, and she said it was a very hard time for them all to get their heads around it and come to terms with the fact that they had a child with a disability.

So, when that little question popped up while I was pregnant, I told Mick I thought we should find out so that we could tell everyone while I was pregnant and so that we could try and get answers to all the questions that we had and research to try and find out what our world would be like. But you don't know…every child is different whether they're mainstream or whether they have a disability, but you don't know that at the time. You think if it's a disability then, BAM!! It's just going to be horrendous.

It was five weeks later when I went to an obstetrician for another ultrasound. I was 15 weeks pregnant and he said a similar thing, "Look, everything looks good. The heart looks good, all the internal organs look great, the baby is a good size and length. The stenographer was right, the thickness of the neck is 2.8mm, so I wouldn't base a diagnosis on that, but I think everything's fine, the baby looks normal." I told him we had talked about it, and I had a feeling that Down Syndrome would be diagnosed at some stage and that we would want to know. He said I needed amniocentesis to be 100% sure, which tests for all different chromosomes, the main one being chromosome number 21, which is the chromosome that indicates Down Syndrome. There's an extra chromosome in number 21 if Down Syndrome is present.

They also tested other chromosomes. From memory I think it's 11, 13 and 17 as well, because there are other chromosomal disorders that can come up. So, a bit of an education there for me, which was good.

Because Mick and I had spoken about it and had decided we wanted to find out for sure, I'd asked him if he could perform the amniocentesis, and how long it would take and when I needed to book in. I had Blake with me. Blake was five years old and was sitting at the other side of the room watching the ultrasound and looking at this new little baby on the screen. He was very excited, his big beautiful blue eyes looking at the screen, saying, "That's our baby! That's our baby!" I still remember that like it was yesterday. It was lovely.

The obstetrician said he could do the amniocentesis there and then; it would only take five minutes. I had to gather my thoughts for a few minutes and think. I wasn't expecting that. I was expecting him to say he would do it in a couple of weeks. In my mind nothing was going to change with or without the diagnosis, we just wanted to know so we could prepare everyone. To me, it didn't matter when I had the amniocentesis, because nothing was going to change with the pregnancy. So, I sat up and I grabbed Blake, and I said "Look, the doctor's going to do another test for the baby to make sure the baby's okay."

Something Is Different

It was pretty daunting and scary, just the thought of what he was going to do. I knew what was involved. I'd read up on it already trying to prepare myself. You can never really prepare yourself though. When people say the words, you tend to go into a bit of panic and think "Damn, I thought I was prepared for this, but I wasn't expecting him to say we should have it now."

I still remember feeling quite petrified at the thought of what he was going to do next, but I was reassuring Blake that everything was going to be okay and mummy and the baby were going to be fine, don't panic, the doctor's not going to hurt us, but in my mind I was terrified. I was thinking, "Oh my God, what am I doing? Should I be doing this test? Should I just not worry about it? I don't want to put the baby at risk, but I want to know."

I had reassured Blake that everything was going to be okay, but I was secretly laying there on the bed, petrified that something was going to go wrong and the baby was going to get hurt because I knew it could be a risk.

The doctor told me that he had a good space where he could take the fluid, because the baby was entirely on the right-hand side of my belly, so he had a massive pocket of just fluid, so he wasn't going to be touching the umbilical cord or going anywhere near the baby.

He approached with the needle. The needle that I stupidly thought was going to just be a normal needle. It was HUGE. It was long and thick and when I looked at it, I thought, "My God, he's going to put that in my belly." When I looked at Blake, he was sitting there with a smile on his face saying, "It's going to be okay, mummy."

So, I took a breath and held onto the side of the bed. The doctor asked if I was ready. Of course I wasn't but I shut my eyes and waited. I was waiting for this piercing, thick, horrifying needle to go into my belly and the excruciating pain that was going to come with it.

I asked him how it was going and what was happening. "It's in," he said. WOW!! I didn't even feel it. I was so relieved. He told me the stomach is a good area for needles. He started drawing the amniotic fluid out, which was one of the weirdest feelings I've ever felt in my life. It felt like he was extracting part of the baby out of my stomach.

Thankfully it was all over and done with within five minutes, and then he reassured me that he would rush the results through. I wasn't worried about getting the results quickly because with or without a diagnosis it wasn't going to make any difference to the pregnancy. We were having the baby no matter what. It was always about finding out so we could let our close friends and family know.

I left his office that day feeling happy we had decided to do the extra testing and quite excited to get his phone call. I walked to the car with Blake without a care in the world. Not worried at all about what the outcome would be.

Something Is Different

CHAPTER 2

VERDICT

The results came the very next day, which was amazing. When he said rush, I thought he meant a week, not the next day. Because I was 15 weeks pregnant, he wanted to get the results through so that I could have the option of going ahead or terminating. At 15 weeks, it's not just a case of termination. There's a lot more involved. It was never an option in my mind anyway.

We were at my mother-in-law's wake when the phone call came through. I think it was about four o'clock in the afternoon. Even though I thought he was going to say yes, the baby has Down Syndrome, my heart started to beat out of my chest, and I started to shake. I went out to the front of the venue and answered the phone. Everything was happening in slow motion. It was very strange. He said, "Look, I'm really sorry to tell you, but the baby has Down syndrome. I'm so very sorry."

I told him it was all right and he didn't need to be sorry. I assured him a couple of times that I was fine, and everything would be okay. All

The Unexpected Journey

the while, inside I was feeling a tremendous amount of sadness and I was doing everything to hold back the tears. We didn't know whether the baby was a boy or girl at this stage. I told him it was still going to be a little baby that was going to come into our family. He told me there were lots of options out there and we'd talk about them more at our next appointment. I was happy with that and didn't really want to talk anymore. The call ended and I composed myself, all the while feeling great amounts of sadness inside.

I remember thinking, why? "Why are you sad? Why are you crying? Why are you behaving like this?" At the same time, I was telling myself that I knew the result was going to be positive for Down Syndrome. But I couldn't help it. I think it was just all the build-up and the anxiety of all the tests, the conversations and waiting for the call. I'd held everything in for a couple of weeks since the first scan, so I think all the emotions just wanted to pour out.

I found Mick and told him what the doctor said. We both started to cry and hugged each other. And then we looked at each other and started to laugh because we were both expecting that verdict and didn't know why we were both crying. We decided not to tell everybody at the wake because we thought that was a bit too much for everyone to handle. The plan was to visit family to tell them and to ring friends.

About five minutes later, my brother-in-law, Chris came up to me and fell into my arms sobbing, saying he was so, so sorry. I asked him what he was sorry about, actually wondering why he was sorry as we were at his mum's funeral.

He told me Mick had just told him about the baby and he couldn't believe this was happening. My strength started to kick in and I kept telling him everything would be fine.

Verdict

After that we decided we may as well tell everybody else. They all knew we were waiting on the phone call and I think I'd told most people I was expecting the doctor to say the baby had Down Syndrome. Despite this, everybody's reactions really shocked us. They were all so devastated and upset.

My thoughts went straight to what Tina had told me. She said this was going to happen, whether it was before or after the baby was born. So, I don't know why we were shocked that they were responding this way. I don't think we were quite prepared for it. So, we went through the motions and told everyone who was there, and by the time we told the last couple of people, we were quite okay about the whole thing.

I kept telling everyone it was going to be okay. I told them if there's a medical issue, today's modern medicine is amazing and there are fantastic schools for kids with disabilities. I was convincing myself as well, but I knew it was going to be fine because of my friend's little girl. Even though she had her challenges, I saw that she was just a little girl wanting to play with other children and I saw she was comfortable in her skin. She went to kinder like other kids and enjoyed it. I kept thinking about that to reassure myself.

When we got home, we got a phone call from our Auntie. I thought she was ringing to tell us it would be fine, and everyone was behind us. Instead, she told me nobody would judge us if we made the decision to terminate. She was worried about the baby and what life would be like and I think she just wanted to let us know they would support us if we did terminate. Nobody would judge us. I told her I appreciated the call, but we were going ahead with the pregnancy and bringing our baby into the world. Of course, she understood that, but I think in her head she just needed to tell us we were supported.

The Unexpected Journey

The next doctor's appointment came around. I was seeing two doctors - an obstetrician who did all the ultrasounds, and a GP who was my doctor through the pregnancy. The first appointment was with the GP. He also told me how sorry he was, how devastating it must be, and then followed on with the options; I could go ahead with the pregnancy, or I could terminate. I told him I didn't want to terminate, I wanted to go on with the pregnancy. I was 15 weeks, and I didn't want to change anything. He told me the length of the pregnancy didn't matter, and termination was still possible. He explained he had a legal obligation to tell me my options and how termination would happen should I decide to go down that road.

I was happy for him to tell me, and I listened even though I wasn't going to terminate. He told me that at this stage of pregnancy, I would be admitted to hospital where they would give me a pill that brings on labour. Then I would give birth to the 15-week old foetus, which is a baby at this point. Because it would be so early to give birth, obviously the baby wouldn't make it. I understood it was his obligation to tell me, but it was the most horrible thing I've ever heard anybody say. He said it so matter-of-factly, but I guess that they have to tell people things like that all the time.

The next appointment was with the obstetrician for another ultrasound. He also told me he had a legal obligation to tell me my options. I explained I had already been told my options by the GP, and I'd made my decision. He told me exactly what my other doctor had told me.

We found out the sex of the baby at these appointments. The letter that you get stating the testing of the chromosomes also states the sex of the baby. We were having another boy! So happy.

Verdict

Now, I highly respect both of these men as doctors and did understand their legal obligation but didn't understand why they felt the need to repeatedly tell me about the termination. The obstetrician was with us for my older two boys, and I loved him to death. I thought he was amazing. They both told me the same options at least four times until about the 20-week mark. My appointments became more frequent when we found out the verdict of Down Syndrome, so I saw them a lot. The doctors telling me so many times was quite distressing. This was a life that we had decided we were bringing into the world no matter how many times they told us we could terminate. This was our little boy that they were telling me I could terminate. Finally, after getting quite distressed at them both, they stopped telling me the options and started treating the appointments like any other pregnancy.

I think doctors need more education on how things are today for a lot of people with disabilities and I think they need to listen to their patients, especially when they are clear on their decision. We're not in the 50s or the 60s anymore. There are many people with disabilities living enriched, full lives…I know some of these people. I think the option should be explained once. Clearly, so people understand, but once only. I think explaining the options repeatedly is a bit like bullying, and they should listen to their patients after they've given them the courtesy of listening to them.

Once we got past that stage, the doctors were quite good. They were supportive of our decision to go ahead with the pregnancy. We decided to have regular ultrasounds just to make sure everything was progressing well. I listened to his heartbeat at almost every appointment and the ultrasound showed his heart was perfect. His other organs all looked fine, which was a relief. This was the first time I had a 3D ultrasound. We saw his little face, his little button nose and all his other features. It was amazing. He was perfect.

The Unexpected Journey

The shock at our decision to find out about the Down Syndrome didn't stop at the doctor's appointments. My next appointment with the hospital doctors at 30 weeks was quite interesting, to say the least. I was booking in for a Caesarean birth because I'd had Caesareans with the other two boys. I couldn't give birth naturally and after Caleb, the decision was made that all my births would be the same. So, I went to the hospital to book in and fill out the paperwork.

I was sitting in the waiting room for about 10 minutes reading a magazine and watching other ladies come in and go out. I thought it was very strange that other ladies were coming in and seeing the doctors while I was still waiting. After about 20 minutes I heard some whispers in the hallway. I didn't think too much about it until one of the nurses popped her head around the corner, smiled and promptly went back into the hallway and started whispering again.

It went on for about another five minutes, when finally, a nurse came into the room to tell me it wouldn't be too much longer. Then back out she went, and the whispering continued. I was wondering what they were talking about, suspicious that it was about me. I was feeling paranoid and becoming irritated.

She eventually returned and when I looked at her, she seemed as though she'd seen a ghost. Her face was as white as a sheet and she looked very nervous. She told me the doctor would be about another five minutes. I said that was okay and went back to reading my magazine. She didn't leave and stood there staring at me. I asked if something was wrong and she told me they could see I'd had lots of ultrasounds and an amniocentesis. I immediately knew what she was going to ask me, but I acted dumb and told her yes, I did have quite a few scans and tests.

Verdict

She asked me if I'd been to see my doctor again after the amniocentesis. I knew what she was going to ask, and I was going to play a bit of a trick on her, but she was so distressed I decided not to. I told her I had spoken to my doctor and the obstetrician after my tests and yes, I did know the baby had Down Syndrome.

The relief in her body language and on her face was remarkable. She was so happy I had been told and that I was okay. She said so many doctors didn't tell their patients the results and left it up to the hospital to talk to them about it. I was surprised because that stage of pregnancy is in the last trimester.

The doctors shouldn't leave it up to the hospital, but as a patient you should be ringing the doctors, not waiting 15 weeks after a test to have the poor hospital tell you what's going on. If I had waited any longer than a week, I would've been straight on the phone to find out the results.

I'd been sitting in their waiting room with a big smile on my face, rubbing my belly, and they were out there panicking, wondering if I knew my child had a disability or whether they would have to tell me and who was going to tell me. I remember going home and telling Mick what had happened. I still couldn't believe it.

I'm glad I didn't tease the nurse about it. It wasn't her fault, especially if most of the time doctors don't give information they should. The relief in her face was a nice moment because she was happy that I'd been told, and she seemed happy we had made the decision to have the baby.

When I was with the doctor, he told me he was glad that I knew the test results and he was happy that we were going ahead with the pregnancy. That was the first time a doctor had told us that. It felt empowering.

I walked out of that room overjoyed that I was bringing this beautiful little boy into the world. It was going to change our lives forever. We didn't know how. We didn't know what was lying ahead for us, but then again, we don't know what's lying ahead for any of us. Whenever we have a baby, we don't know what's going to happen once they're born, when they're at school, when they become adults. Anything can happen at any time. Any challenges. Sometimes they're big, sometimes they're small.

But to me, it felt as though the changes this little boy was going to bring were going to be good. Probably some challenges along the way, but I just had a really good feeling. I had a feeling he was going to be an amazing little soul.

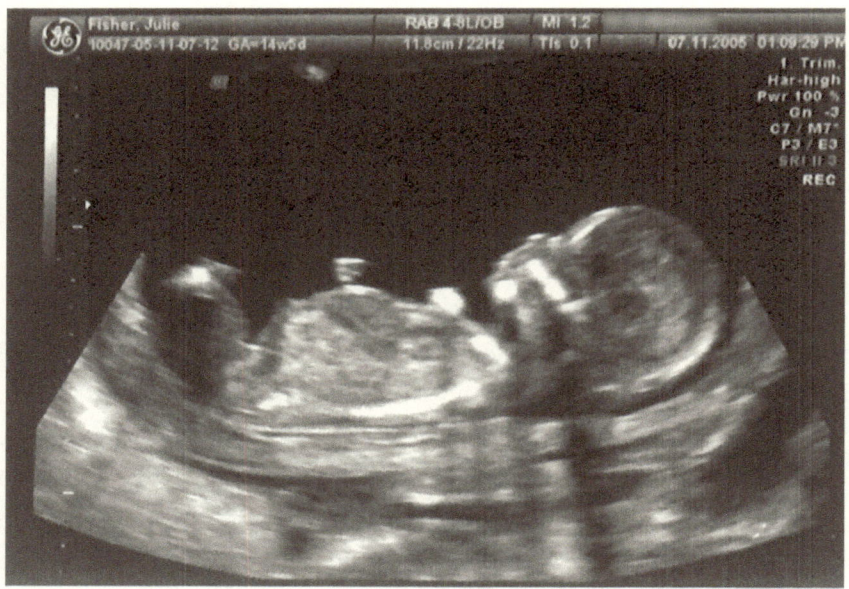

Verdict

INTERPHASE FISH REPORT

LabNo:	2051107.02
Specimen Received:	07-Nov-2005
Patient ID X 2:	Yes
Report Issued:	08-Nov-2005
Days to Final Report:	1

33 Cranbourne Road
LANGWARRIN VIC 3910

Patient Name: Mrs Julie FISHER
34 Monze Drive
LANGWARRIN VIC 3910

Contact Phone: 97757058

DOB: 15-Feb-1969

Cells Counted: 50
Specimen: amniotic fluid
Result: nuc ish Xcen(DXZ1x1),Ycen(DYZ3x1),13q14 (RB-1x2),18 (D18Z1x2), 21q22.13-q22.2(D21S259,D21S341,D21S342x3)

ABNORMAL FISH REPORT

Interphase FISH analysis of uncultured amniocytes was consistent with a trisomic chromosome complement of chromosome 21 and a normal complement of chromosomes 13 and 18 in a male fetus.

Full cytogenetic analysis will follow.
Note: Probes used are from the Vysis Aneuvysion Assay Kit

☐ NO FURTHER ACTION
☐ CALL PATIENT
☐ URGENT REVIEW BY / /
☐ NON URGENT REVIEW BY / /
☐ APPT MADE

(Senior Scientist)   (Cytogenetics)

(Pathologist)

RECEIVED 10 NOV 2005

cc: 9783 3030
BY: ....

CHAPTER 3
CYCLE OF GRIEF

When you find out you are having a child with a disability, grieving is quite natural, and it seems to come out of nowhere. I think it's because you think you're missing out on that normal, perfect child and all of a sudden you feel like you're entering an unknown world. The perception of what is normal is something we all grow up with. We don't want anything to be wrong with our children.

Health issues are another concern and cause for grieving. You also worry about what other people are going to say and think. Such as, why are they doing this? We shouldn't worry about what other people think, but I think it's just a natural instinct sometimes. I was so happy and looking forward to meeting our little man, but the grief just kept making its way into my mind even though I thought I was fine. Silly thoughts that just pop up unexpectedly.

I think everybody who comes into this world has got something to bring to the table. Something to teach everybody. But nevertheless, you still grieve. I guess it's because you're worried that things aren't going to go how you planned.

I seemed to go in and out of those emotions, which confused me most of the time. I went from grieving to celebrating. Up and down, up and down. I remember looking at Caleb and Blake and wondering what this third little wheel was going to look like. Would he be like them? Probably not. He probably won't talk. He probably won't walk. He probably won't want to do anything. He probably won't want to play. I don't even know where those thoughts came from, they just appeared.

I'd met Amy and I could see that she walked and played. And though she wasn't verbal at the time, she could still let her mum know what she wanted. It was hard for others to know what she wanted, but her family knew. And even though I could see that she did these things and wanted to join in, I still sat there and thought he would probably be a lump on the couch. Or a lump on the floor. How would we cope with that? How would we teach Caleb and Blake how to deal with that?

I remember getting angry sometimes wondering why this was happening to us. Why is this happening to our family? Why can't we just keep going along as we are with our perfect little family? I have boys playing sport. This next little one coming along probably won't want to do any of that. He won't want to go to the park. And what if I want to take Caleb and Blake to a movie? I won't be able to go. These are the things I was thinking when he wasn't even born yet.

They were just natural thoughts that used to pop into my head at random moments. I could be out shopping and I'd just get a vision of this baby, just this lump in the shopping trolley with no emotion. I don't know why I kept thinking that.

Cycle Of Grief

When I was growing up, we didn't see a lot of people with disabilities. By the time I was pregnant with Darcy, you saw many people with disabilities. When I saw people with disabilities shopping with their carers, I remember watching them to see what they did and how they communicated. It was awful because I found myself staring a lot of the time. I didn't mean to stare; I was just curious to see their behaviour.

I remember thinking one day, we weren't going to have any more children. And then we got the false alarm which made us decide, yes, we would have another child. So, it was meant to happen. The Down Syndrome was meant to be a part of our family. And we had to start embracing that. But I think when you put pressure on yourself to do that, you grieve a bit more, like forcing it. That's what it was like for me.

Silly thoughts still kept popping into my head like, will he like toys? What a silly thing to think; of course he will like toys. I also had thoughts of his brothers not wanting to do anything with him. I thought they would just ignore him. What if I don't like the way he looks when he's born? What if I look at him and I don't want him? I was petrified of that. Absolutely petrified that I was going to look at this child and not want him. That was my biggest fear. I didn't tell anybody about that until after he was born. It consumed my mind.

I kick myself now for thinking like that, but I think it was part of the process, part of the not knowing. Not knowing what he was going to look like. Not knowing what he was going to be like. Even though I knew he was very healthy, so really, he was perfect. We were bringing a healthy baby into the world. Yes, he had a disability but, he was healthy. He had nothing wrong with him internally. He had all of his limbs. All of his fingers and toes. Two eyes. Two ears. His breathing looked normal in the womb. Everything was right.

The Unexpected Journey

He was perfect. And he was normal. But he had Down Syndrome, so how could he be normal? Grief is such an overwhelming thing. And it's really hard to understand. Especially when you are grieving the upcoming birth of a child. It's just a process you go through, I guess.

Watching family around us, they were all so worried. They used to look at me with such worry in their eyes. "How's the pregnancy going?" "Really good, everything's normal. Had another ultrasound and the baby is doing well, growing well."

But everybody was grieving. The boys were grieving too but because they were so young, they just sort of went with the flow. I tried to always be positive about it in front of them and always smile about it. I always talked about how exciting it was going to be. They helped with the room and to pick toys and clothes and things like that. So, I guess to them it was all normal and they were quite happy. But I think when they saw other people with worry in their eyes, they didn't understand. They were only eight and five while I was pregnant, so it was a bit hard for them to understand grief.

I wanted them to be excited about the baby coming and having another little brother. Caleb already knew what it was like to have a little brother, so he was really excited. And Blake was just excited because he knew babies were cute and did funny things and he was going to have a little brother to play with. Moments like that made me happy and took away the grief. They made me excited about bringing him home.

And then when the boys were at school, I would sit there and start worrying again about silly things. Will he be able to see? Where does that come from? I don't know.

Cycle Of Grief

What sort of things am I going to do with him? Is he going to like the same things that the other boys liked? Probably not, I kept telling myself. He probably won't like nursery rhymes and singing and reading books. I still bought special books just for him and toys, and all of the same sort of cute clothing that the other boys had when they were babies. And then I wondered if it would matter. He'll never care about what he wears. All of these stupid thoughts were going through my head, over and over and over again.

The grief consumed me sometimes, taking over all of my thoughts. I couldn't help it. You can't help but grieve over something that you think isn't normal or perfect. As soon as we think its bad news or something we're not expecting, something that we think is going to be challenging, our mind goes into automatic pilot and starts worrying and grieving and stressing. A few times I remember seeing people down the street with kids with disabilities and looking at the children and thinking wow, they look happy. Look at them; they haven't got a care in the world. Then I'd touch my belly and think, God I hope this baby is going to be like that. Please let everything be okay. And then I'd look at the kids again and think it is going to be okay.

Then that other little voice in my head would fill me with doubt. They look happy but that doesn't mean that my baby is going to be happy. Strange thoughts went through my mind whenever I went to the shops. But I soldiered on. I pushed through and kept trying to push those negative thoughts to the back of my mind and push the positive thoughts of a new baby, a new life, a new beginning to make us a family of five. Well, actually six. I cannot forget our gorgeous Bree. I remember telling her, and she was quite fine with the whole thing, saying, "Oh well, that's wonderful. I can't wait to meet him." Gorgeous girl.

The Unexpected Journey

As the pregnancy progressed, I managed to succeed more at focusing on the positive. The grief used to sneak back in every now and then, but then I'd see something, and I'd push it back. Or I'd look something up to ease my mind and put the positive thoughts back.

I started going to my friend Tina's support group, which was great. The women I met, and their gorgeous kids, really helped me to stay positive about what was going to happen to us. Because at the end of the day, we were bringing a little boy into the world. A little boy that we had named Darcy. It wasn't going to be a bad thing. It was going to be an amazing thing. I couldn't wait to have the baby so that all those thoughts, the wonder, the not knowing could be pushed away because once he was here, I wouldn't have those negative thoughts anymore.

I knew that was going to happen because I'm a mum already. I've got two boys, I know how to look after kids. So, I couldn't wait to have him so that this horrible grief that kept popping into my mind would go away forever. I didn't like it. I didn't want to have it. I just wanted to enjoy my pregnancy and the impending arrival of little Darcy.

I just wanted that grief to go away. But it's a natural process. We all go through it at some point in our lives, I guess.

In hindsight, I wish I knew what I know now because those extra emotions wouldn't have been there. The worry still would, because we all worry about our children from the moment they are born and for the rest of our lives.

If I knew what I know now, I would know there isn't anything wrong with people with disabilities. They are just different, and we are all different anyway. It broadens your ideas when you enter the world of disability.

Cycle Of Grief

A man once asked me, "what is normal?" I asked him what he meant, and his answer was, "normal is a setting on a washing machine." I have never forgotten that, and I quote him quite often when I speak to people.

CHAPTER 4

DEMYSTIFYING DOWN SYNDROME

After the diagnosis and trying to come to grips with everybody's reaction and all of the grief and negativity we were hearing and thinking, I decided to get in touch with my friend Tina who has her little Amy.

Caleb and Jenni, Tina's eldest daughter, were having a concert at the school, so the first step in trying to help everybody move forward with the diagnosis was to ring my friend and ask if she was taking Amy and her husband to the performance. If she wasn't, I was going to ask her if she wouldn't mind bringing them because I'd like Mick to meet her husband and Amy, so that he could see what a cute little kid she was, rather than just see the Down Syndrome.

Tina did bring Chris and Amy and that night, after the concert, we all met up and Mick got to meet them and chat with Chris. Tina and I were just talking and noticed that Amy took quite a shine to

Mick. She didn't talk a lot, but she's quite a character and Mick really enjoyed that interaction with her. She was being very cheeky, which was great for both of us to see. When we got home, everything was quite positive. We started talking about how exciting it was going to be for Darcy to arrive.

As I mentioned, Tina also ran a support group once a fortnight at her house. I met many other women with children with Down Syndrome, as well as children with other disabilities. All the kids were quite little, not many of them were at school and a couple of them were babies. I loved watching the mums with the babies and seeing how they interacted with them. They seemed to care for them exactly the same way I had cared for Caleb and Blake when they were babies. It was very normal. I remember thinking that to myself because of all the negative thoughts I had been having.

It was great listening to the mums' stories. Some were stressful, some were happy, but I remember sitting there one day thinking, a lot of the stories that they're telling me are things that my other two kids have gone through as well. Behavioural problems at certain stages, trips to the hospital for gastro and pneumonia, etc. I got to see that the kids with disabilities were different, but they weren't at the same time.

And they still did all of the same things that other kids did, reached all the same sort of goals, but at different times, just like other kids. Some take a very long time to reach certain goals, but at the end of the day, they were reaching them just like any other kid. It was nice to listen to these stories and tell Mick. I really enjoyed those fortnightly catch-ups. I learned a lot about what was going to happen when Darcy arrived; the things I needed to do, things I needed to book for him, and it gave me a really positive outlook.

At Christmas time, Tina had a family barbecue for everybody, so I invited my dad and step-mum. I really wanted them to meet some of these people. Some of the other children's grandparents were there too, and it was great for them to connect with them. It didn't matter if they were going to have long-term friendships with these people or not, I think it was important for them at the time to talk to other people and listen to their stories about how proud they were of their grandchildren, just the same as any other grandchild. They really enjoyed being there and watching all the kids. A wonderful part of it all was watching Caleb and Blake play with the kids as they did with their friends at school…no different at all. I remember my dad turning to me and saying, "Have a look at them all. They just play, just like Caleb and Blake do." I said to him, "Yeah, I know, it's pretty cool, isn't it?" It was good for all of us to see they played and squabbled just like every other child we knew.

All of the things we had started doing were a real turning point for all of us, because we started becoming more productive getting ready for Darcy. We were a lot more positive, rather than clinging onto all those negative thoughts. It's funny though because I also remember having negative and worrying thoughts about Caleb and Blake while I was pregnant because things were going to be different. Worrying if I was going to be a good mum. So, I guess when you think about it, whenever something new and different is coming, worry happens.

Once at the group, the women were talking about the length of their pregnancies, and the majority had their kids early. That scared me, and I remember thinking, "Oh God, I don't want to go too early." I was already booked in at 38 weeks because I needed to have a caesarean. The panic I felt was quite intense, and I started to worry about going early but telling the baby to wait until the due date. As if that makes a difference!

I took the advice from other parents to book things early so that I didn't have to go on waiting lists once Darcy had arrived. The waiting list could start while I was pregnant. So, I booked the early intervention at Biala in Mornington for the date he was due. I also rang my paediatrician that we'd had for the older boys and made an appointment for a week after his due date. I liked him a lot when he looked after the other boys, so I knew I wanted him for Darcy. I felt organised and on top of the world having those two things booked.

I also got in touch with Down Syndrome Victoria, who were great. They sent me some information with lots of tips to get through the process of grieving and dealing with any questions that may arise. They also offered to put me in touch with other people around Victoria who run the groups like Tina was running. I told them that I knew Tina and had already started going to the groups. They were pleased that I'd put myself in contact with support so early. They also run lots of workshops that you can attend both in the early stages and as the children get older and advice for help along the way.

All of that was great for me, and I think the most important thing for Mick was meeting Chris, Tina's husband. I think for him it was like the support group for me. He could vent to him about how he was feeling, because I don't think he wanted to upset me too much. I don't know why he thought I'd get upset if he had negative feelings, because I was having them too. Surrounding yourself with people who are affected by disability and have disability in their homes and their lives and in their hearts is good. I think if you connect with people like that straight away, it's extremely helpful. Even when you listen to the stories that are a little bit daunting, it's still good to hear because they worked through them as a family and got through it.

Demystifying Down Syndrome

I started to realise these families were just like any other family. These children had the same feelings as everybody else. That was a big thing that I learned. They might not be able to verbalise it clearly, but I could see, meeting these other kids that they knew what was going on, they knew what was right and wrong. They knew when they were hungry, when they wanted to go to the toilet, they knew everything that they wanted to do. And somehow, some way, they got it across, whether they were verbal or not.

And that was really cool to see, because it gave us a lot of hope while I was still pregnant with Darcy. And it helped Mick to be more positive about bringing this little guy into our family. Because it was quite daunting, not knowing what lay ahead. It's funny how you think you don't know what's ahead, but really at the end of the day, you do, because you're having a baby. Pretty much that's it. They might have some extra health issues, or they might not. They might need extra time learning how to feed, or they might not. So, it's just like any other baby really. You worry about all that anyway, hoping that everything is going to be okay, hoping that they're going to be healthy.

We knew that Darcy was healthy, which was a huge weight off our shoulders. It was phenomenal. Having those extra ultrasounds all the way through the pregnancy just to make sure that everything was staying on track were really beneficial and helpful. At the end of the day, we knew he had a disability, but he was healthy, and he looked perfect. He looked like the other boys on the ultrasounds; a little baby. And that's what I kept saying to Mick and everyone else around us. Mick came to the ultrasounds when he could, which was positive reinforcement and a great coping tool, because he could see that our baby was doing fine.

The Down Syndrome seemed to become less of an issue as my pregnancy progressed. Even though we were talking about it all the time and surrounding ourselves with people who had disability in their lives, it sort of took a back step. For me it did anyway, and it became more about the baby. I enjoyed that because I could then start focusing on his room and toys and clothes, and I stopped worrying about silly little things like what he was going to play with. Of course he was going to play with the same things other babies play with.

Going through that process and meeting all those people was great - for Mick, our family, and for me - because it put me in a place where I was concentrating on the baby more than the Down Syndrome. And whether that was because I was able to book appointments and such for after he was born and I could get that out of my mind, I don't know. Whatever it was, I started focusing on the baby and not the disability.

And that's what I wanted to do. I wanted to focus on the person, on who he was and who he was going to be. He was going to be our little brother, our son, our last baby. And I wanted to enjoy it. I wanted to enjoy the pregnancy like I did with the other boys. I didn't want to stress and worry all the way through. So, linking in with the supports was wonderful.

We got to enjoy the pregnancy as just that, a pregnancy with the wonderful ending of having a new little person in our lives.

3D scans had come in when I was pregnant with Darcy, and this helped me immensely. I got to see the shape of his face and all his features. It was amazing. It really helped me to see the little boy and not his disability.

After all, that's what he was…a little boy.

Demystifying Down Syndrome

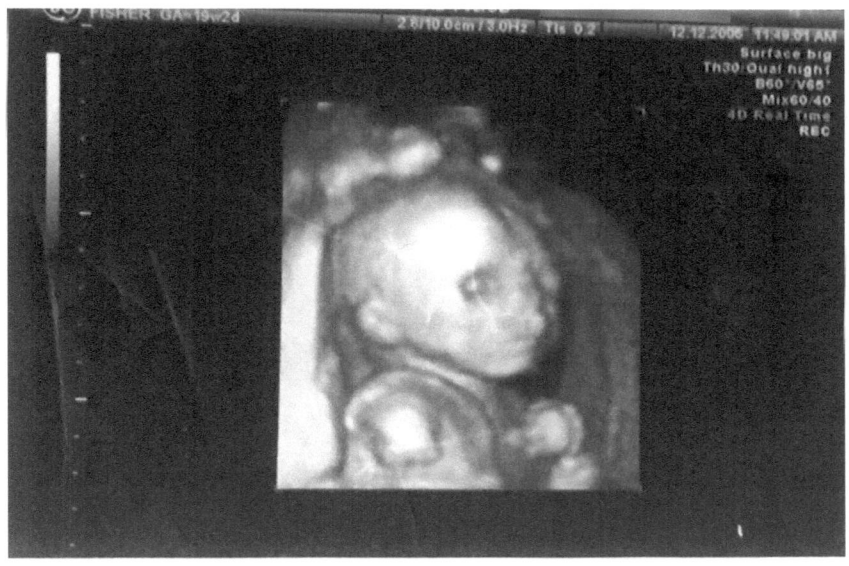

The Unexpected Journey

CHAPTER 5

GETTING READY FOR THE BABY

After weeks and weeks of wondering, heartbreak, happiness, and all kinds of emotions, the countdown was on. His due date was 3 May which was five weeks away, but I was booked in to have him on 29 April.

I went to the coffee group, and all the ladies were talking about the early arrivals of their kids again. I remember quietly sitting there wishing they would stop talking about all that. I felt they were putting the mozz on me! While they were talking about it, I felt as though they were looking at me as though I was about to go into labour any second!

I didn't want to have the baby yet. I wasn't ready. I hadn't even organised anything to take to the hospital. I hadn't packed a bag. I had the suitcase out, but I hadn't packed it. And I just remember sitting there listening to them saying, "Oh, I went six weeks early."

"I went four weeks early." "It's okay, and it ends up being fine." I was panicking inside my head. It was too early! He was going to have enough challenges ahead let alone being born early. I told them all it wasn't going to happen to me, and they would all get to meet him after 29 April. I was trying to push positive thoughts into the situation while I was quietly worrying, I could go any minute.

That afternoon while walking home from school with Caleb and Blake, a girlfriend drove past and beeped her horn at me. She rang me when she got home and asked if I was okay because she'd noticed my belly had dropped incredibly and looked like I'd had it and it was time. I told her I was okay, just tired. I reassured her the baby was going to stay put for the time being and not to stress. She said instead of walking everywhere, I should be putting my feet up. I kept assuring her I was fine and there was nothing to worry about. The whole time in the back of my head I just kept thinking, please not yet. Here was another person talking about going early.

Anyway, I threw a few things in the bag just in case. Not much, just a couple of things like shampoo, deodorant, a T-shirt, and a pair of pants. I only put a few things in because I still was sure I was going to go to my due date. I just thought I'd start getting the bag ready so if any more conversations went the way of early arrival, at least I could say I was organised and had started packing.

The next day when I woke, I was repeatedly on and off the toilet. I started making the kids' lunches ready for school, and back on the toilet I'd go. This happened about six times. I secretly knew exactly what was happening because it happened this way with Caleb. I decided to go into denial.

Mick sensed straight away there was something going on. I told him the baby must be pressing on my bladder because I couldn't stop going

Getting Ready For The Baby

to the toilet. I still remember the look on his face when he asked me if my waters had broken because that's exactly what had happened with Caleb. There was no gush of water, just the feeling of needing to go to the toilet all the time. I told him no it wasn't my waters, it was just the baby pressing on my bladder.

In my head I was stressing out because I needed to go to the shop and get a few things for the kids' lunches and get them organised for school. I still had lots of things to do for the baby's arrival as well, so this couldn't be happening.

So, off I went, running around the supermarket thinking I needed to go to the toilet again, but knowing it was my waters because my pants were soaking. I needed to get this done so the kids were organised and there were things at home for when I went to the hospital.

I finally got to the checkout after what felt like hours running around the shop, and the lady at the register looked at me and asked if I was all right. By this stage, I was standing there thinking, the next stop is Frankston Hospital. I'd felt my pants, and I was wet from my waist to my knees. Yep! My waters had broken. I told her I was pretty sure my waters had broken. I've never seen anyone move faster to get me on my way back home. She told me she couldn't believe I had come shopping. I kept thinking about Caleb and Blake going to school and what they needed.

She got me out of the supermarket in super quick time and back home I went. I walked inside and told Mick my waters had broken. PANDEMONIUM! Mick went into panic mode and started working out what needed to be done. School clothes and bags ready, half-packed hospital bag closed and ready at the door. I didn't even think about what was in there, just that it needed to come with me.

The Unexpected Journey

The kids were still in their pyjamas, running around full of excitement. We rang Tracey and Brian, who we had organised to take the kids to school when I went in to have the baby. She started to panic as well because she knew I still had a few weeks to go.

We dropped the boys off to a very excited McCartney house, and then we headed to the hospital. Tracey was reassuring me as we left that everything would be okay and not to stress. Easier said than done.

Later that day I spoke to Tracey and she told me the boys were so good. Caleb, the eldest, (he was nine at this stage) told her he was worried because it was too early, "what if something happens to the baby?" With tears in her eyes, she told him everything would be okay, and the hospital would look after us. Little Blake, who was six, looked up at her full of excitement and said, "we're having a baby!" He was so excited. He had no concept that it was early and that everyone else was freaking out. One was worrying and one was super excited.

On arrival at Frankston Hospital they confirmed my water had in fact broken. The stage of pregnancy I was at was 34 weeks and five days. Because of the Down Syndrome diagnosis and because we were under 35 weeks, they told us they didn't want to take any risks with birthing the baby there. If there were any complications, they weren't equipped enough to deal with it, and we would have to be rushed to a larger hospital.

The decision was made to transfer us to Monash in Clayton before the baby was born. That way, we would arrive safe and once he was born, if there were any complications, they would be able to address them.

The ambulance arrived and off we went. I had never been in an ambulance before and I was feeling very nervous and scared. It was

Getting Ready For The Baby

so strange in the back there, laying down and travelling along. I felt a little car sick which hadn't happened since I was a child. I wasn't enjoying that feeling but it took the panic away from the impending early arrival of my baby.

We arrived at Monash and I can't remember where the room was, but they sat me in a big recliner to try to keep me comfortable. We were still waiting on Mick to arrive while they were monitoring me and trying to keep me calm. Labour had started so they told me because I was five weeks early, they were going to try and stop the labour to delay the birth for as long as they could and as long as my body would allow. The next thing, I had a needle shoved into my leg. Not even a minute later, the labour pain stopped. The pressure of the baby pushing down had stopped. A couple of hours later and once Mick had arrived, they put me in the maternity ward in my own room. Time for rest and wondering when this was all going to start again.

They were very good at Monash and checked me regularly. Every professional who saw me had a student with them, so I was speaking to many different people. The midwives, anaesthetists, obstetrician and paediatrician all had students with them. I think it was because of the knowledge of the Down Syndrome before birth. It was interesting having all those people around. Watching the professionals listen to me without batting an eyelid, and watching the students, wide-eyed, taking everything in. It was very busy, and I was exhausted. I remember just lying there at one stage wishing they would go away so I could rest. I wanted a couple of hours of sleep because there was a lot going on in both my head and my body that was wearing me out.

When it came time for Mick to pick the boys up, he was worried about me, but I told him I would be fine. I think he was worried that the baby might decide to come while he was gone but the hospital was certain we had at least saved one day. Time for sleep while he was gone…I needed it.

The boys came and saw me that night. I had a good amount of rest and there was still no signs of labour. The baby was pretty settled, and his heartbeat was still normal. Everything was good with me as well and it was so good to see my boys. Blake was a little disappointed we didn't have a baby yet, but I told him, good things come to those who wait.

I was settled in for the night and then BANG! At 2am I woke to severe pains. Labour had started. I sent Mick a message to let him know and to come straight after dropping the boys at school the next day.

The rest of the night I was in and out of sleep with labour pains coming and going. Because I knew I couldn't give birth naturally and they wanted me to go on for as long as I could, I knew the baby wouldn't be here before at least lunch time. It was nine hours of intense, hard labour, and I was really struggling. The doctor came in and I remember looking at him saying, "Please, you have to stop this. I can't do this anymore. I just want to have the baby." Another needle went into my leg and the pain stopped. The labour didn't, but the pain did. I don't know what it was they gave me, but I didn't argue about it.

They had booked me in for the caesarean at 1.30pm but when the doctor came in again, he could see I was really struggling. He ran out the door and straight back in telling everyone the time was here and to get me going now. There were people running around everywhere. I just remember laying in the bed, my head spinning. I was happy because I knew that it was all going to stop, and we were going to have our little boy very soon.

Getting Ready For The Baby

Mick had come in after dropping the boys off and was with me through the whole thing. I needed him there and was relieved it was a school day. At roughly 12 noon, down we go to the operating theatre. Once again, knowing about the Down Syndrome before Darcy was born, there were students with all the professionals. It felt like there were 100 people in the room. It was very full and very busy with an unbelievably good vibe. Everyone was anxious to see the little boy who had caused so much curiosity. I was quite happy to have the extra people there; they need to learn somehow! Everyone was interested throughout my whole pregnancy because I knew about the Down Syndrome. The questions I was asked were amazing, including some I would never have thought of.

The birthing started with the caesarean, which felt like a lifetime. I was worried he would have trouble breathing straight away due to being so early and because both Caleb and Blake needed help to start breathing. They were born two weeks before the official due date so I was sure Darcy, who was five weeks early, would need help. Boy was I wrong. When they pulled him out, he was screaming. He didn't need any assistance at all, which we were so relieved about. There didn't seem to be any problems with his lungs and the whole room erupted. It felt like being at a rock concert! Everyone was cheering and clapping and seemed so happy that he was here. It was a real celebration. It was beautiful.

I remember looking at him while he was being held up in the air and being so proud. He was going to make his mark on the world, and I couldn't wait to get my hands on him. They quickly wrapped him up, and in a flash, he was on my chest. I was in love. He was perfect.

I remember panicking before he was born, worried about what he would look like and that I may not want him. When I looked at him,

The Unexpected Journey

I couldn't believe I'd had those thoughts and instantly felt guilty. I still feel guilty 13 years later about feeling like that.

"Isn't he beautiful?" I said to Mick. He was a gorgeous little boy. He was perfect. Our little boy was born, and our family was complete.

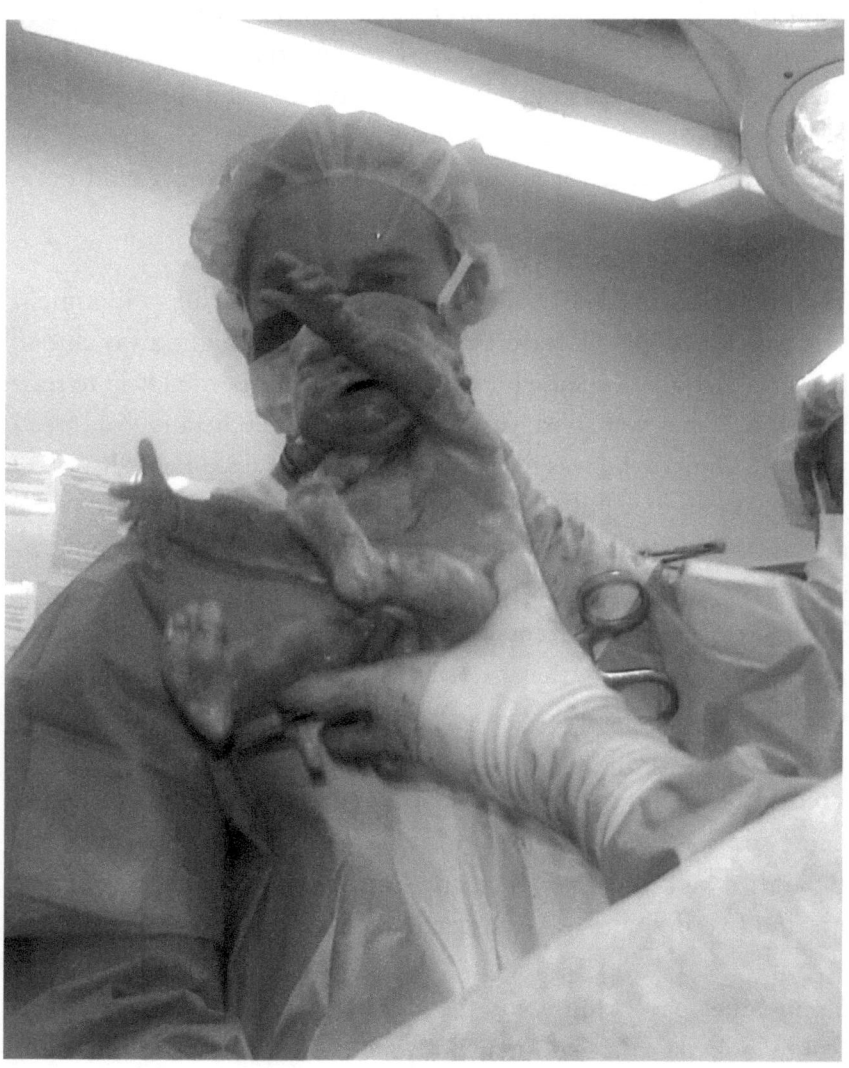

CHAPTER 6
HE'S HERE

Finally, our special little boy was here. We were so happy that he didn't need any help to breathe; he did it all on his own.

Like the other boys, having him on my chest and Mick and I getting to meet him was such an amazing moment. I remember looking at him thinking he was just like the other two boys. I was expecting him to look really different, but he didn't. He looked exactly like he belonged with us. It really was a wonderful moment.

We both just stared at him with such pride, happiness, relief and gratitude. Grateful that he was here and healthy, and grateful for all the staff that were there. They were all so supportive and positive. I really needed the positivity because leading up to this moment, there were so many different emotions running through my head.

Once we got to say hello to our little man and have photos taken, off he went, and I had to go into the recovery section of the hospital.

The Unexpected Journey

He went to the NICU at the Monash Hospital special care nursery. I went to my room and got some more well-needed rest, so I didn't get to see him for a few hours after he was born.

I wasn't allowed out of bed for 24 hours because of the caesarean. Once I'd woken, all I wanted to do was go and see him, so I was extremely frustrated. Eventually, and after much complaining by me, they worked out they could wheel the whole bed with me in it around to the special care nursery. Excited is an understatement of how I was feeling. I couldn't wait to see exactly how big he was and get a good look at all his beautiful features.

They told me he'd already had a couple of feeds and was doing well. When I saw him, I couldn't believe how tiny he was. He didn't seem that tiny when they put him on my chest wrapped in blankets. He was 2.2 kilos, or in the old scale, 4lb 14oz, and 44 centimetres long. The tiny little newborn nappy that he had on didn't even fit him properly. It was folded down, almost in half, so that it didn't hit his chin. I've kept one of those nappies so that I can remember how little he was. I get it out every now and then and am always amazed at how tiny it is and how little he was. I don't remember him being that small.

He was in a humidicrib because he had slight jaundice. Nothing to worry about, they said. I was feeling so overwhelmed laying there looking at him. All I wanted to do was hold him and tell him everything was going to be all right. I remember looking at him, sound asleep with this huge nappy on him, with lights and a few monitors on him, thinking how perfect he was. He was beautiful, a gorgeous little boy. He had a little bit of hair and tiny little hands and feet. He was sleeping so peacefully. There he was, our special little boy. It was an incredible moment.

He's Here

The next day, I was allowed to get out of the bed. They still wouldn't let me walk, so they took me to see him in a wheelchair. This time we took Caleb and Blake with us. They were beside themselves with excitement.

He was out of the humidicrib and had moved up to the next room. They move rooms in stages of progression at Monash. From memory, the room numbers started at 9 and went down to 1. Room number 1 was closest to the door to going home. He had moved from room 4 to 3.

We were allowed to hold him. It was the best moment. The boys bathed him, did his hand and footprints and helped dress him. I loved watching the boys with him, and they loved doing things with him and helping. They looked so at ease while doing all these things with Darcy, yet I felt so awkward. It had been six years since I had done anything with a baby, and I think because he was so small, I felt like I was going to break him. I'd forgotten what it was like to do anything with a baby and started feeling a bit useless. The nurses were very supportive. I think if it weren't for them, I would've given up for a couple of days. I kept thinking, I'm his mum and I can't do anything with him.

I think it was a little because of the Down Syndrome because the muscle tone is low, so they can be quite floppy. Once I gained my confidence, I realised he wasn't too floppy, which the doctors and nurses confirmed. They told me just to be a little extra careful with his head. Picking him up for the first time I struggled to remember what the other boys were like when they were first born. It had been six and nine years since they were born.

Family and friends started coming in on day three. I was expecting everyone the day after he was born but nobody came in. Stupidly, I thought it was because of the Down Syndrome. Mick had told everyone to wait an extra day so we could get a bit of rest. He didn't tell me that until afterwards.

Day three he had lots of visitors and was spoiled rotten. So many photos were taken, and we have so many wonderful memories to look back on. Watching everyone look at him with such love was such a special moment. He didn't realise what an impact he was already making on everybody and neither did we, but he was amazing right from the start.

All of our kids are incredible, and they all have their own special qualities, but Darcy seemed to have something extra special. Even with his brothers. He was a real little miracle. He had something special about him, but he wasn't really all that different. He looked and behaved like a normal baby.

All that worry, grief and stress throughout the pregnancy, and here he was, just a baby that needed to be changed and bathed, and wanted to be fed and loved, just like anybody else. And that's exactly what he got.

The best visitors to me were Caleb and Blake's friends. They were all so young, but when they came in and held him, they all looked like big brothers who were going to look after him for a very long time. They all looked so proud and I remember thinking he will always have someone looking out for him for the rest of his life. He had so much love right from the start.

We spent the next week at Monash. He was doing really well. Feeding well, growing well. His hearing and heart tests all came back with good results. It was time for me to go home and I was hoping he would be coming with me as he was doing so well. But Darcy needed to stay in special care for a little while longer. I was devastated. I wanted him home or at least closer to us. I was dreading travelling to Monash every

He's Here

day, so they were trying to get him a bed at Frankston Hospital. They weren't having any luck and I was really starting to get distressed. I'd been discharged from my room, but I didn't want to leave him.

After trying for 24 hours, they were starting to think they weren't going to be able to get him into Frankston for at least another week. The emotions inside of me were so hard to cope with. I was pretending to be so strong but breaking inside. I wanted my little boy close to me. We tried to work out what was going to happen each day travelling into Clayton and making sure I was also home for Caleb and Blake. We went to say goodbye to Darcy before we went to pick the boys up.

As we got to his room, they told me they had some news. They had a bed at Frankston for Darcy, and they were just waiting on the ambulance to arrive to transport him. I was so relieved and because I was so emotional, my legs just crumbled from under me, and I started to cry. They thought I was upset, but I told them I was so happy that all my emotions just poured out.

We stayed with him until the ambulance arrived. It was a specialised ambulance and Darcy was on his belly, which I panicked about. They explained when babies are being transported, it's the best position for them. There would be someone in the back with him to make sure he was okay. They were so gentle and careful with him, and they really looked after him on the trip.

Off we all went – the ambulance to Frankston Hospital, and us to pick the boys up. The boys wanted to see Darcy straight away, so we went straight to Frankston. They were fantastic at Monash, but it was so much better having him closer to home. The nurses at Frankston were great too and the nursery was lovely.

After three weeks in special care, Darcy could finally come home. We had a beautiful room set up for him, and everyone was buzzing with excitement. He fitted in straight away as though he'd always been there. I think the boys got out every toy he had, trying to get him to play. The animals were curious, wondering what this little thing was. They weren't used to something this small that didn't move around a lot.

He was so tiny, even the 00000 clothes were too big. He was putting on weight, but very slowly. Just little bits at a time. We put that down to the Down Syndrome. We just figured that because of the low muscle tone and slower development, his growth would be slower. We weren't worried.

While he was in the special care nursery, his oxygen levels went down sometimes. There didn't seem to be an explanation about this, and the nurses and doctors just thought it was the way he breathed. We didn't think anything more of it and trusted their judgement. He was monitored constantly and never seemed to go blue or struggle breathing.

He came home on the day I was booked in to have him. We were so pleased with this because originally, they didn't think he would be home until the five-week mark after his birth. Not having to go to the hospital every day was fantastic. I loved the nurses and felt safe with them being there because I was feeling quite overwhelmed having a new baby six years after my last, but I was so happy not to have to go there anymore.

Pretty soon, routine started happening - popping him in the pram, going to school, going to the maternal health nurse, shopping, doctor's appointments, visiting friends. It felt great because it was all the same things I had done with his brothers.

He's Here

The first time I took him to the school to pick up the boys was quite a shock because when I got there about 20 women rushed over to look at Darcy. It was very overwhelming and felt like there were about 100 women there. Most of them were friends who were excited to see him and full of congratulations and lots of love. However, some of them were acquaintances just having a look. I remember hearing a lady say, "Oh no, I just wanted to see what he looked like." I remember thinking wow, what sort of comment was that? My immediate response was, "He looks like a baby." She got embarrassed while everyone laughed and then they all left.

That was my first encounter of a negative comment towards Darcy. I didn't like it at all and wondered why someone would think it was acceptable to say something like that. Especially an adult. I think I responded the right way, but it still upset me. He was my son, not something for people to stare at. I seemed to be able to push it behind me and move on.

Life was very busy with Caleb and Blake at school, as well as having basketball and football every week and training and games on the weekend, but Darcy settled into the routine really easily and seemed to enjoy being home. He was sleeping through after the second night at home. I couldn't believe it but was very grateful. Everything settled down and our life went along beautifully.

He was home where he belonged.

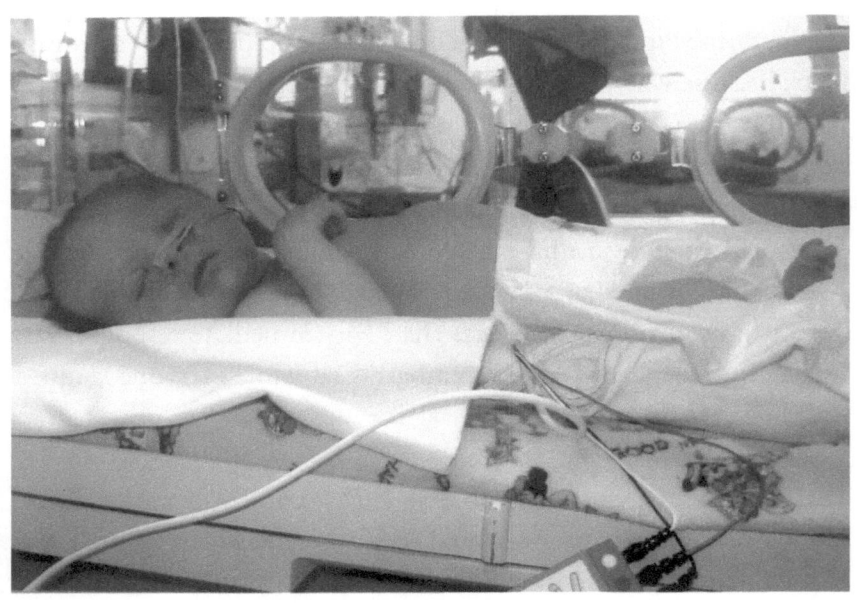
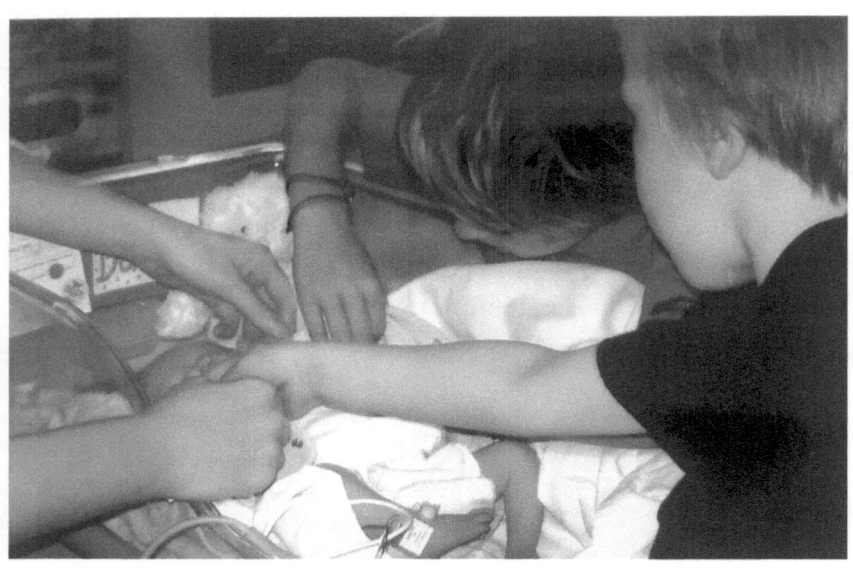

He's Here

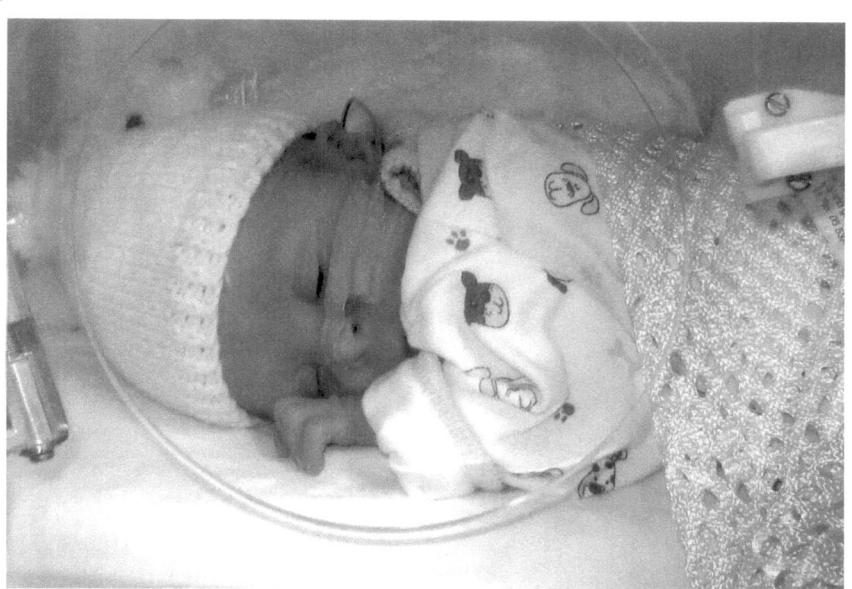

CHAPTER 7
EMBRACING UNCERTAINTY

Darcy was a very placid baby and very easy to look after. We started having our appointments with the paediatrician, and everything was looking good. He was healthy and his heart sounded great, which was number one because a lot of kids with Down Syndrome have complications with their heart. It was really nice to not have to worry about that.

The kids adored him. They were always touching him, holding him and offering to help. "Can I help feed him?" "Can I help change him?" "Can I bathe him?" I loved that. It really brought us together even more. It was a different special kind of bond.

We started seeing the maternal health nurse. She'd never looked after a child with Down Syndrome before, so she did a lot of research and printed out a special growth and height chart because they have a different one. She said if we used the mainstream one, it would seem as though he was never reaching his goals. So, having the Down Syndrome specific chart showed that he was on track. His doctor loved it and told me he'd never had one before. Thinking back, I actually think he said that to make me feel better because I was so happy she had found it.

We started at Biala in Mornington; early intervention where they help with skills like sitting, eating, walking and talking. There was an OT, speech therapist, and physio. There was lots of sensory play, singing and nursery rhymes encouraging them to do things. We learned massage for them, which Darcy loved. It was very relaxing for both of us. We went every Wednesday morning and met some lovely people, some of whom are still friends today. The kids had different disabilities and were all just as amazing as the next baby. Darcy really seemed to enjoy going, and so did I. It was a great way to connect with more people who were going through similar things as we were.

He started Biala when he was four weeks old, a week after he got home. We were able to start so early and not go on a long waiting list because I was able to book in while I was pregnant with him. My friend Tina knew Darcy would need early intervention and recommended I book in early.

Having Tina really helped the whole time with my fear about Down Syndrome. Right from the time we found out and once he was born. She had been through it all before and made me feel like it wasn't anything extra we were doing. She made me feel like it was just part of the things I needed to do with my baby, nothing extra special at all.

I was still worried and uncertain about milestones and other things like that. I knew that it was all going to come a bit later, but how much later? Joining the group and going to Biala was good for me for things like that. It helped me see that even though milestones would

Embracing Uncertainty

come at very different stages to his brothers and other kids, it wasn't anything to worry about. All kids reach their milestones at different stages. Caleb didn't walk until he was 15 months old, whereas Blake walked at 12 months old. It didn't mean it was a bad thing or that he wouldn't reach them.

As time went on and he started to grow, we started concentrating on trying to get him to stand. We'd stand him up in a corner leaning against the wall. He was so proud of himself and happy that he was standing. He knew it was a good thing because of all our cheering, encouraging him to try to stay there.

His sensory issues weren't too bad, but one thing we did have to work on was sand. He hated sand and there was no way he was going to let us get him into the sandpit. Every week we would try, without success. He was little but boy he was strong, and we just couldn't manage to get him in.

We decided to carry him into it one day. I had his legs and Jane, the physio, had the top half of him. He thought this was fun until he realised where we were taking him. For a kid that had low muscle tone and was supposed to be floppy he was so strong, and it took everything we had to get him in and onto the sand. When we finally got him into the sandpit, he looked at me as if to say oh, that's actually not so bad. In an instant he went from being scared to loving it and eating the sand. Even though I didn't want him eating sand, I was so happy we had finally achieved this goal.

I think this was the point where I decided that I would always persist with things with him. If he was unsure or scared, I would talk to him about it, make small steps towards the goal, and eventually he would see it was okay. If it doesn't work the first time, try again. Persistence to show him things would be all right and nothing bad would happen. Persistence so he could see things would be fun and enjoyable.

Sitting on his own took a while and I think he was almost one before he accomplished this. There were lots of assistive things we used to help him and so he could see how good it was rather than laying on the floor. Crawling came a lot later, and that was a hard milestone to teach. We ended up using a ball to encourage him to come to it and eventually it worked. I think he was almost 18 months old. His favourite thing to play with has always been a ball, so we've used a ball a lot for encouragement.

As he got older, the want for him to achieve his goals became more and more. Uncertainty was there for when these would come and also what to do to encourage it. I wanted him to be able to do things on his own and trying to work out strategies that worked was hard sometimes. Biala and the therapists helped with that, but all the children were different. What worked for one didn't always work for the other. It really was trial and error.

He started babbling around the same time as his brothers so I was certain he would be verbal. I made the decision not to encourage sign language with him and only learned basic signs. I spent a lot of time talking closely to him, mouthing the words slowly in an attempt to try to make him see properly and say things. I just had a gut feeling that he would talk.

So, I talked to the speech therapist, and while she didn't discourage me, she did want me to learn the sign language. We agreed I'd learn basic sign and she would come up with some ways to help encourage the speech. We were all happy this way.

Embracing Uncertainty

It's daunting and scary, but when they're your child you just seem to find the strength to do the extra things and help them get to where they should be. I remember being worried about Caleb and Blake meeting milestones too, so I just tried to think it was no different. Even though the ages were very different, I was still teaching Darcy like I had taught his brothers.

At Biala, it didn't feel like the kids were different at all. They were all reaching milestones later than their siblings and at different times to each other. They enjoyed nursery rhymes and musical instruments like any other child. Lots of things they did were just like other children. That was what helped us to go on and not get tied up in what they couldn't do. It was the beginning of learning to focus on what they could do.

It was interesting watching the parents and kids and watching everything unfold. Some of the kids didn't like the music, some of them didn't like the musical instruments, some of them hated the messy play and some didn't like eating and drinking.

Darcy loved the music and the musical instruments right from an early age, so I knew that was going to be a strong point for him with encouragement for a lot of things. We always promoted that sort of thing with him, music and singing, and before too long he was singing songs himself. So, every week we went to early intervention and watched him start to achieve new things each week.

Little did we know at the time, but singing was going to be a vital tool in his speech development. We are always singing around the house, so the combination of Biala music and music at home proved to be very important in this development.

The Unexpected Journey

The uncertainty was always there, though. Thinking back now, I think it was probably more fear of him not accomplishing milestones because I wanted him to. I wanted him to be able to do things like other kids and I wanted him to enjoy things with his brothers as he got older. When he was a baby, there was that fear that wasn't going to happen. There was the fear that he might always just be on the floor, because it took so long for things to happen. It's normal to feel like that, and it's not bad. But you just have to keep working at it. Working at it with them and believing in them, and constant encouragement.

They're our kids and we want the best for them. They deserve it.

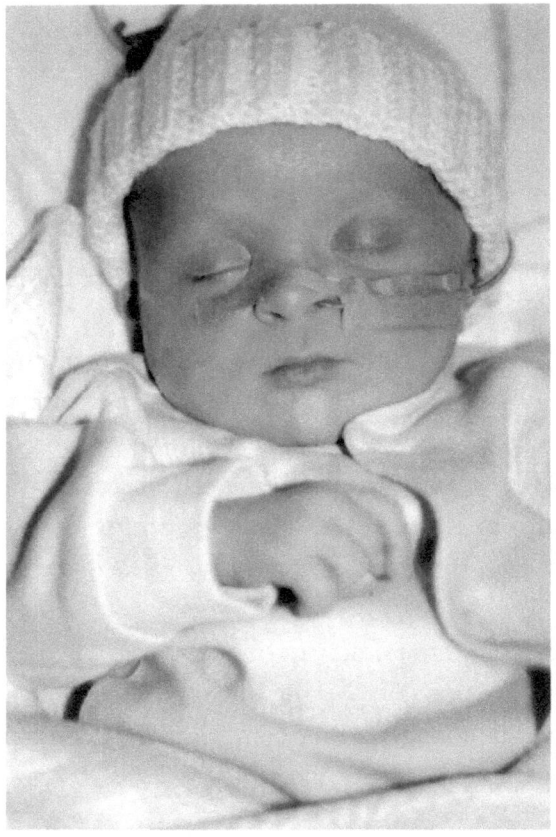

Embracing Uncertainty

The Unexpected Journey

CHAPTER 8

BEYOND COMPLICATIONS

Once we got Darcy home and started all the paediatrician appointments, early intervention and all of the things we needed to get him moving and thriving, we finally started to relax and get into a bit of a routine. He had a good sleeping pattern as soon as we got home which helped with getting into good habits and getting things done.

Suddenly though, one Sunday afternoon he started vomiting every bottle I fed him. Pretty much as soon as he'd finished and I sat him up, it just came straight back up. I was trying so hard to be positive and tell myself he was just having a bad day, but I was terrified when bottle after bottle, they came back up. I started remembering when Caleb was three weeks old and the same thing happened. He ended up needing a double hernia operation and I was starting to think that this was the same thing. Darcy had no temperature and had seemed fine until the vomiting started. It went on for about four feeds, but after the last one, I took him straight to the hospital.

He was taken straight into the emergency ward and into a bed. He'd started to become dehydrated because he couldn't keep anything down. I told them the symptoms and that he hadn't been crying or upset, didn't have a temperature and had seemed happy.

They started him on fluids to rehydrate him and then the waiting started while they observed and monitored him. They wanted to know if he had diarrhoea, because they thought it might be gastro, but there was nothing like that. It was just the vomiting. That was the only sign. And it was quite scary because he wasn't a child who cried or became distressed. He was a very relaxed and happy child, who never complained or cried for anything.

After about six hours, the doctor told me they thought it was gastro and asked if I was happy to take him home. He told me to try and keep his fluids up in smaller amounts and see how we go. It seemed to me like he didn't have any idea and wanted to free up the bed.

I wasn't happy to go home. I was quite frightened because I didn't want anything to happen to him where there weren't any resources to help him. We were seeing Dr Lowther, his paediatrician, the next morning at 9:00, so I went home only because of that.

When we left, the nurse who had been looking after us told me if I became worried not to come back to the hospital, but to ring nurse on call. She told me they were extremely busy, and it would be best if I didn't come back there. I was pretty annoyed at that and couldn't believe she had said it. Thinking back, I should have reported her for such unprofessional behaviour.

Beyond Complications

We went home and I tried to give Darcy smaller feeds and he seemed to be okay. He ate and slept but also had a few more vomits. They weren't as bad as the earlier ones, but that was only because he was getting smaller feeds.

The next morning, we went to see Dr Lowther. I told him what was going on and what had happened at the hospital and that I was quite worried because there didn't seem to be anything wrong except for the vomiting. Ted, being the very calm man that he is, did Darcy's weight and measurements, checked his chest, ears and throat and had a little chat to Darcy. I was starting to think Ted thought there was nothing wrong apart from a little gastro and then he asked me to just sit there with Darcy on my lap. He made some notes and looked up at Darcy every now and then and asked me to go over everything that had happened once again.

He looked up once he'd finished his notes and asked me to tell him what colour I thought Darcy was. I looked and told him I thought he looked very pale but thought that was because his little body had been through a lot of trauma with the vomiting. Ted told me to keep calm but said that Darcy was actually grey and wasn't breathing properly. He said it sounds like he has fluid on his lungs.

I went into a panic, wondering what was going on. Tears were welling up, but he told me not to panic and that he was sending us straight back to the hospital. He told me they would be ready for us and would have a bed very quickly.

He called them as we sat there and told them what had been going on with Darcy. He said he had possible aspiration and fluid on the lungs. What did that mean? I don't think he explained that to me at the time because he knew it would panic me even more.

The Unexpected Journey

We immediately went to the hospital emergency, and because of Ted's call, we were let straight in. As Ted had promised, we got a bed straight away. The nurse who was there to look after us was the nurse we'd seen the day before. She was very shocked to see us, and I was very quick to tell her that Darcy was very sick. She obviously had no words to say to me about that. We ended up with a different nurse and I was happy with that. I think if she had have stayed looking after us, I would have said something. I still to this day don't understand how she could have spoken to me like that about my boy who I was terribly worried about.

Then the waiting began. They were taking his temperature, hooking him up to things and I wasn't really sure what was going on. I was so worried about my little man and I just wanted this nightmare to be over. I wanted them to fix him so we could go home again.

We got a bed in the children's ward that afternoon and again, doctors were coming and going, as were the nurses. Ted came to see us and told me after listening to Darcy's breathing, he was sure it was aspiration that was causing the problems. I really didn't know what that meant but it didn't sound good. He explained that some of what Darcy was drinking with his bottles was going onto his lungs instead of into his stomach.

After some x-rays they worked out that it was about a half-half ratio. Half was going into his stomach which was why he was slowly gaining weight, and half was going into his lungs. Ted explained to me that aspiration was when whatever you're eating or drinking goes down the wrong hole and you choke. Normally when people aspirate, they start to choke and cough. We didn't know this was happening to Darcy because he wasn't choking or coughing. They call that silent aspiration and it is very dangerous. We were really lucky that Darcy had started vomiting otherwise it would have kept happening and eventually he wouldn't have been able to breathe at all.

All of this information was mind-blowing. It was so much to take in. I was so thankful we had that appointment with Ted and that he was so assertive in getting us back to the hospital. Mind you, if I hadn't had that appointment with Ted, I would have stayed at the hospital the day before. I knew in my heart it wasn't gastro.

Now that we knew it was aspiration, Darcy needed to see a lung specialist. Ted recommended David Armstrong but unfortunately, he had quite a long waiting list. From memory it was six months. But they put a referral in to him and Darcy went on the waiting list.

Darcy was in the best place and being cared for very well. He had to have oxygen to help clear the fluid in his lungs, start breathing properly and he had a nasal gastric tube for his feeds. The tube goes into the nose and down into the stomach. That way, the feeds bypass the throat and go directly into the stomach.

I wasn't allowed to hold Darcy while all this was going on so that they could monitor his breathing properly. It was so hard. I remember always having a hand on him, stroking his head or his back and holding his little hands. I learned how to do the nasal gastric feeds and how to monitor the oxygen.

A couple of days later when the doctors were doing their rounds, we saw a lovely paediatrician, Anne O'Neill. She noticed Darcy was on a waiting list for David Armstrong and told me he was her husband. Grinning at me, she went into the hallway to make a phone call to David. The nurses were motioning to me that this was great. I heard her tell him about Darcy and that he should come and see him today.

The Unexpected Journey

Apparently, he had a day off and was playing golf. He would come and see Darcy that afternoon.

Lady luck was on our side. The nurses said what great news it was, and Darcy would be able to start getting treatment a lot quicker than originally thought. He would jump the waiting list and was going to start seeing him immediately.

They told me David Armstrong was brilliant and would be able to work out everything that was going on very quickly and start Darcy on the road to recovery.

My head was spinning with everything that was going on with Darcy, as well as constantly thinking about Caleb and Blake and keeping everyone informed with what was going on.

We met David Armstrong a couple of hours later. He was a tall man, very confident, friendly, calm and matter-of-fact. He asked me what was going on, listening to me but all the while looking at Darcy. He didn't check Darcy, just watched him and told me about aspiration and what we should start doing while we waited for some tests. He said to start trying him on solids to see if he could tolerate food. That way he would still be using his mouth and swallowing and wouldn't lose the ability to do that. He said if he couldn't eat orally, he would lose that skill and would have to be fed another way permanently. If he could tolerate the solid food, the ability to swallow would still be there and that would be extremely important in the future for him.

We started him on some solids straight away and he reacted very well and seemed to tolerate that. It was only liquid he was struggling with. David watched Darcy eat. He said he thought it may be because he has low muscle tone so his tongue wasn't able to grasp the liquid quick enough to direct it correctly into the right tube so it would end up in his stomach. He said when Darcy was having a bottle, the liquid was falling down his throat without any direction and that's why some of it ended up in his lungs.

He was so calm when telling me everything which helped to calm me down and focus on what needed to be done to help him. It made me see that he was going to be all right.

We had to have a videofluoroscopy to confirm what David thought was right. This is where they put a radioactive solution into the feeds and x-ray while Darcy was drinking. They started it with normal thin liquid and then added thickener to see when he could tolerate the liquid. We were hoping he could tolerate a thick liquid so he could still have his bottle feeds. Unfortunately, he couldn't tolerate any of the liquid, so the nasal gastric tube had to stay.

I think we were in hospital for about one and a half weeks. Now that they'd worked out everything that was happening, they told me it was best to take him home. I was really nervous because he was hooked up to oxygen and I was worried about the nasal gastric tube coming out. I didn't want to have to put the tube in by myself because I was worried I wouldn't get it into the stomach. Because it was going to be the way to feed him for some time, we all decided a PEG (Percutaneous Endoscopic Gastrostomy) would be the best thing for Darcy. A PEG is a flexible feeding tube that is placed through the abdominal wall and into the stomach. It allows the feeds to go directly into the stomach, bypassing the mouth and throat.

I called the hospital on the morning of the day he was coming home and spoke to Andrea, a nurse I'd spoken to often. She had become very fond of Darcy and asked if she could keep in touch with us once he came home. She also had a daughter with Down Syndrome and had spoken to me about her. I was delighted she wanted to keep in touch, so of course I said yes.

She was our angel. While we were waiting for the surgery to give Darcy the PEG she would come and reinsert the nasal gastric tube when it came out. That was such a blessing because otherwise we would have had to have gone into the hospital to have it done. We got special permission for her to be able to do this. We became good friends and are still friends now, 13 years later.

Darcy was on oxygen for a couple of months while his lungs repaired. We got very used to taking it everywhere with us and it became almost normal. I was very happy when we were told he was breathing well, and we could take him off it. He was happy too. No more tubes in his nose apart from the feeding tube.

We were on a waiting list for the PEG for a couple of months. In this time, we had repeated visits to the hospital when things would start playing up again. His breathing would go up and down even with the oxygen, so in and out of the hospital we went. It had started becoming quite normal for him to be in there.

He was going between Frankston and Monash almost every time we visited the hospital. Frankston was great because it was so close to home and the nursing staff were second to none. Monash was great because David Armstrong was there and could come and see Darcy daily. That was the only thing I liked about being there at that time. He made me feel confident every time he came to see us. He reinstated the fact that even though it didn't feel like it, Darcy was improving, and it wasn't going to be like this forever.

Beyond Complications

We were in Frankston hospital when the date for the PEG insertion came up. They transported us in an ambulance to Monash for the surgery. Again, I started to panic and got quite emotional. I liked the nurses at Frankston and wanted them to come with us. Silly really, but I wanted something familiar and I trusted them. I cried when we left, and they assured me we would be looked after well.

Darcy was eight months old when we had the PEG inserted.

Mick was with me and we were so worried about him going in for surgery. They let us go into the prep room with him. They put him to sleep with gas and then we had to go. That was one of the hardest things to watch…Darcy all of a sudden going limp and falling asleep. The team there were incredible at making us feel okay to leave him with them and assuring us he was going to be okay.

It seemed to take so long while he was in surgery. Finally, he had finished, and we could go into recovery to see him. We were shocked when we saw him because he had the needle that would normally be in the back of his hand in his head. They couldn't find a vein anywhere in his hands or arms, so they put it in the vein in his forehead. I don't know about Mick, but I was horrified. They reassured me it was okay and wouldn't be in for long. As soon as he was awake and responding well it would come out.

The PEG area looked a little red but nice and clean. It was a little rubbery, plastic thing with a big long tube coming out. That's what he had for about three months while the site healed. We were given an elastic netting that went around his torso to keep the tube from hanging down.

When the three months was up, he went back into hospital and had it changed to a button that you can open and close. It was flush with his stomach and much easier with dressing and bathing.

The Unexpected Journey

It was such a frightening time. Even when the doctors and nurses were reassuring us, it was very emotional and so many different thoughts were going through our heads. The boys were worried about him and always asking if he was going to be okay. He had spent more time in hospital than at home and they just wanted their brother back.

During that time in and out of hospital, the Nursing Unit Manager at Frankston came into the room to talk to me. She shut the door and asked me if I had any questions. I told her I didn't think I did because everyone explained everything in a lot of detail. She asked me again and when I said the same thing, she said, "Well I am going to tell you the answer to the question you're too scared to ask." She looked me straight in the eye and said, "He's not going to die". The relief I felt was overwhelming and even though I didn't realise it was a question I wanted to ask, it was something that was in the back of my mind. She told me he was getting the best care and we knew what was wrong and it was getting sorted. It was very confronting but something I needed to hear.

It was so good to finally have the PEG and be at the other end of this nightmare. We finally got to take our little man home again, and this time we knew we could stay there without having to make mad dashes to the hospital.

Now we could start becoming a normal family again, with all our kids at home. We now had three extra appointments to add to our yearly list with dietetics, David and the gastroenterology team. Just more people making sure he was okay, so I didn't mind.

We saw David for about 12 months until he was confident Darcy's breathing was staying at a safe level. I remember when he told me he was discharging us, I was quite sad because he was such a great doctor. Very good at making you feel like what was going on was just something that happens sometimes. He made us feel that it was never life-threatening, just a little bump in the road. I was happy we were moving on, but I enjoyed our appointments with him. He made me feel confident with what had happened, and safe.

The dietetics and gastroenterology teams were six-monthly visits to start with, then changed to 12-monthly visits or whenever we thought we needed to see them. Those teams were also very encouraging and always made us feel safe with what was going on.

As Darcy grew, we would have to go back in to have a larger PEG inserted. The PEG needs to be able to spin around (a little like an earring). When Darcy started to grow, the PEG would become tight. The changes seemed to happen every 18 months. We became very used to these PEG changes and it was just something normal that Darcy had to go through.

For now, we were back home getting back into the routine we needed to be in and enjoying being a family at home without having to go backwards and forwards to hospital.

The Unexpected Journey

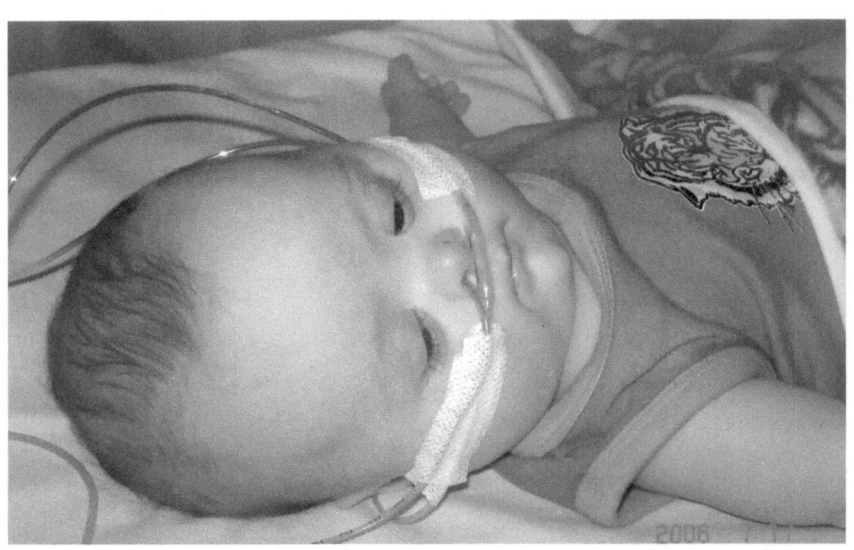

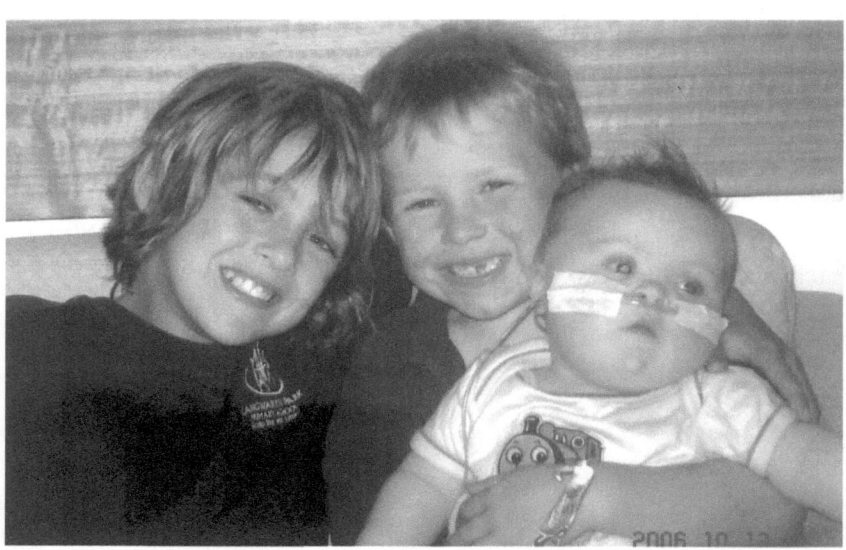

Beyond Complications

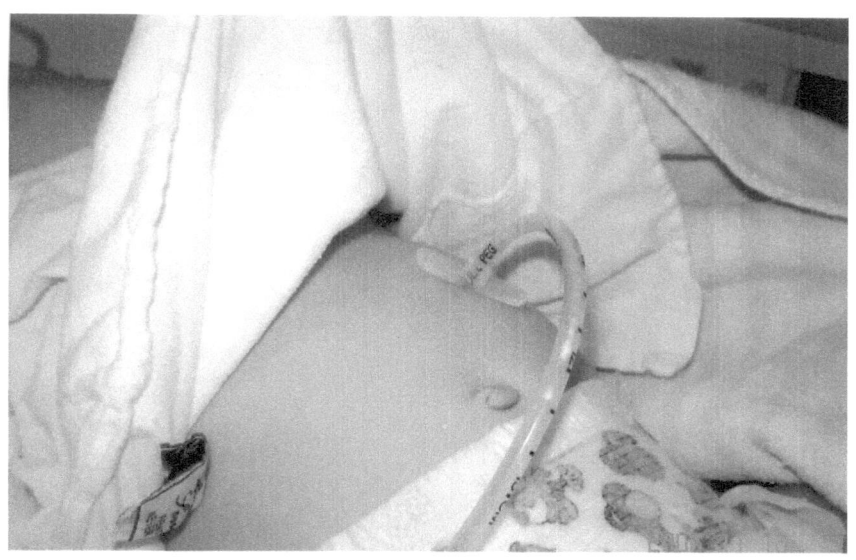

CHAPTER 9
PART OF THE TRIBE

We had our boy home, everything was in order and we were back to family life. Busy going to the boys' basketball and football, birthday parties, school and many other wonderful things.

We knew what we were doing with the PEG feeding. What was daunting to begin with was becoming part of the daily routine without even thinking twice about it. The feeds were three times a day initially, plus the solid food. He was really starting to enjoy his solid feeds and we were able to start giving him more and more different foods. That was such a relief and we were all so happy he was thriving. The doctors were happy with his progress as well and were also quite surprised how quickly he was taking to everything. I think they thought he would take quite a while to start eating different foods. I don't know why they were surprised, and I never asked them. I think I just figured it was because of the Down Syndrome and low muscle tone. They weren't concerned, just surprised. They were very happy with how he was growing and how well he was coping with our busy routine.

The Unexpected Journey

We did a lot each week. Auskick on a Sunday, Caleb's football game, two basketball trainings, two basketball games, school, swimming, as well as Darcy's things. Darcy never complained and just seemed to accept what we were doing and came along very happily.

He was starting to become quite a little character and he really enjoyed watching his brothers do everything. Finally, he was a normal part of the family without hospital stays. He was our son and brother and we were all enjoying being home together.

Everybody embraced him and accepted him for who he was. Our friends and the kids' friends included him in everything, which was important for us and for the boys. Lots of their friends had younger siblings and Darcy was treated just like them - Caleb and Blake's little brother. They played with him just as they did with the boys.

We had family photo shoots, birthday parties, visits to friends', shopping trips, days out and all the normal stuff that families do. That's exactly what we wanted. We just wanted Darcy to be Darcy. We didn't want him to be known as our Down Syndrome son and brother in our family. We just wanted him to be him. We all had our own identities and characteristics and he was no different.

Everyone encouraged him to reach his milestones. It was no different from the other boys. Friends and family would visit, and games would be played; they would stand Darcy up and try to help him take steps. Exactly what happens with any baby in any family. And that's exactly what we wanted. It was wonderful watching everyone treating him just the way they would treat any other child.

The milestones were later than his brothers, but they still came. He first sat up at around 10-11 months. It was a different world for him to be able to sit up and watch everything, play with his toys and his brothers. Crawling started at around 18 months. If he thought sitting up was good, he was amazed at how wonderful it was to move around without any assistance. Caleb commando crawled for a while before crawling on his hands and knees, and Blake scooted around on his bottom before he started crawling properly. Darcy commando crawled for a short time and then scooted around on his hands and knees. We all celebrated these milestones…it was so exciting to finally have him moving around.

As a parent, you're very happy and proud when kids reach their milestones and there are textbook ages of when they should roughly reach these milestones. You are extremely proud of all of your kids when they start learning and accomplishing new things and when you've got a child who reaches them a lot later than other kids, the pride is huge. Maybe because you've been waiting for so long and the feelings build up more. Once he was crawling well, we started trying to teach him how to stand up and learn to walk by helping him stand and teaching him how to hold onto the table and other pieces of furniture. He used to laugh and think it was a game, but he enjoyed it and started trying to do it on his own.

It was taking such a long time. He mastered the skill of standing while holding onto furniture and especially loved it when the boys would help him up. We were beginning to get quite concerned and worried that he wasn't walking yet. At this stage he was three. I had very high hopes of him attending mainstream kinder and I didn't think that would be possible if he wasn't walking.

We discussed extra physio and OT to get his limbs stronger and tried many different things. We had a harness that would go around his body with straps that I could hold onto. That way I would stand him up and walk behind him trying to encourage him to walk. I felt really awkward and I think Darcy could sense that. It wasn't very successful.

While I was feeling quite devastated about it, all my friends and support kept telling me he would walk eventually and to keep persisting. They told me it was one of the hardest milestones they had to teach their children. I remember Caleb taking quite a while to walk so I hoped that Darcy would get there.

We kept persisting with different exercises and aids to help him but none of them seemed to work. I had to hide my feelings about how upset I was. Thoughts went back to when I was pregnant and thinking he may never walk. I know it's not the end of the world, but walking would open up so many more doors for him.

We spoke to Ted, our paediatrician and he suggested a walker - a frame that the child steps into and holds onto. It has four wheels and is very easy for the child to use. While they're holding on, they start to move forward, and the walker goes with them, encouraging them to step forward. It sounded exactly like what we needed.

The walkers were very expensive though - from memory, between $600-$700. This was a HUGE problem as we did not have that sort of money just laying around.

Research into what we could do to try to get the walker led to me finding out about Anglicare, an organisation that had funding windows during the year where you could apply for different types of aids.

The paperwork was relatively simple and the only other thing I needed was a letter of support from Ted, which he was more than happy to give us.

Part Of The Tribe

I wanted to speed the process up, so I lodged the documents in person. Also, this way I knew they had what they needed.

It took about four weeks before we heard our answer and thankfully it was yes. We were elated. This walker sounded like the perfect thing for our little boy and it would definitely stop the worry that had built up again.

It didn't take long for us to find a walker and even though I don't think Darcy really understood what it was, he was excited because we were.

The first time he stood into it, he just stood there looking at everyone wondering what to do. I thought he would stand into it and just start walking and was a little worried when he didn't do that.

After a couple of days, and lots of encouragement from us and his brothers, Darcy started walking with his aid. That opened up so many doors for him. He loved walking around the shopping centre and the whole community came to know him at this stage and they loved watching him achieve his goals. He was quite the speed demon with his walker and people loved watching him scoot around everywhere.

Once he started on the walker, there was no stopping him, often outside playing with his brothers and friends in the street. It was lovely to watch everyone include him in their games and encourage him. There were quite a number of kids in the street we lived in and to them he was just another kid to play with.

He was definitely part of the tribe now that he could do almost everything that everyone else was doing. Fitting in extremely well and enjoying life.

The Unexpected Journey

Part Of The Tribe

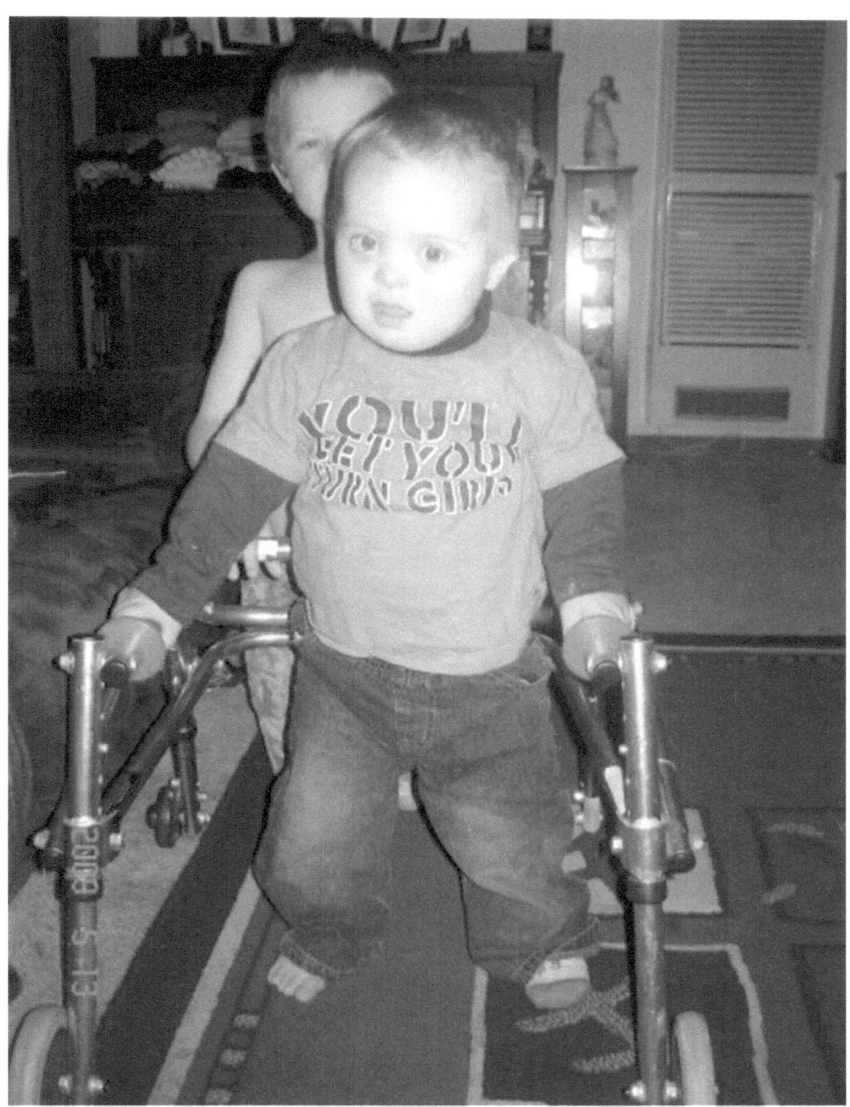

CHAPTER 10

NEW NORMAL

I had lots of things planned for Darcy before he was even born. Knowing his diagnosis before birth and being able to join the support group and see what everyone else was doing with their children was such an asset for me.

Not everyone in the group had babies. Some of the kids were school age. Some went full-time to special school, some did dual schooling, and some did full-time mainstream. It was really interesting listening to everyone talk about these things and how the kids were progressing.

The special schools helped the children with OT, physio, speech and life skills. I thought this would be really important for Darcy and liked the sound of it. I also loved the sound of the mainstream schooling where the kids were challenged a little more and accepted into the community.

For me, even before he was born, I liked the idea of dual schooling because I thought he would get the extra support he needed at special school as well as learn the same things his brothers did at mainstream school, including the experience of camps, excursions and all the same graduation things like the jumper, scrapbook and special school photo. I thought this was important for all the boys.

We finished at Biala at the end of 2008 and Darcy started EEPS (Early Education Program) at Frankston Special Developmental School in 2009. He was two years, 10 months. He did one year full-time and the following year he did EEPS as well as 3-year-old kinder at Langwarrin Park Preschool. His brothers went there, and I was so happy that he could go there too. He was doing four days at SDS and one day at kinder.

The Government don't offer funding for 3-year-old kinder so I did some fundraising so we could hire an aide for him. He wasn't toilet trained and he also had his walker. He needed additional help with fine and gross motor skills, so an aide was important.

Fundraising started with show bag selling at our local school's market night. It was so successful, and we sold almost all of them. In Langwarrin we were very lucky to have Dame Elizabeth Murdoch as part of our community. We approached her to request assistance with some funding. I wrote a letter and the kinder teacher, Kaye Hall, also wrote to her. With our combined requests, she donated $2,200 towards his assistant. She wanted updates on how Darcy was going, and I made sure I supplied her those throughout his 3-year-old-kinder year. With those combined fundraising efforts, we had enough to hire someone to help Darcy.

Our beautiful friend, Blake's 3-year-old kinder teacher, Helen Schwieger offered to be Darcy's assistant. I couldn't have been happier. She was amazing. She'd retired from teaching but was happy to work with

New Normal

Darcy one day a week. That was our first year of schooling and it went so well. He loved both SDS and Langwarrin Park equally and it was no problem getting him to either.

His teachers in EEPS were Jeannie and Marianne, who were brilliant. He had these lovely ladies for two years in EEPS and they were more than happy that he was attending mainstream kinder. They were very compassionate and understanding and you could see that they loved their job. They nurtured the children and were also a great support for us as parents. The two years with them were very enjoyable and we could approach them with anything.

The teachers were fantastic at Langwarrin Park Preschool. I always encouraged the parents to ask whatever questions they wanted. I wanted them to get the right answers. I wrote a letter at the beginning of the year for the teacher to hand out to the parents so they could see I was happy to answer any questions. I thought the letter was a good way to break the ice. Most of the parents came and spoke with me and told me the letter was great because they did have questions and weren't afraid to ask now. I also told them to encourage the kids to ask whatever they wanted. I wanted them to understand that even though Darcy needed assistance, he was just like them. He loved to play. He loved to have friends and he loved to sing and dance just like they did. I continued to do that each year as he progressed along the mainstream route.

As the 3-year-old-kinder got to the midway part of the year, we had to start thinking about 4-year-old-kinder and work out his enrolment. The Government had funding for 4-year-old-kinder but because we were also at SDS, we couldn't have funding for both. That was called double-dipping. What a quandary. I wanted him to stay at Frankston SDS, but I also wanted him to be at Langwarrin Park

The Unexpected Journey

Pre-School because he would be following some of these children into primary school.

We didn't want to ask our community for more money to hire someone because they'd already contributed enough for the current year.

Kaye Hall looked at the enrolments she already had, and we decided to sit tight for a little longer to see what would happen with them. She assured me it would work out. We would come up with something. She was amazing and made me feel less concerned about it.

I wanted him to stay at Frankston SDS because that's where he was going to be doing the bulk of his schooling once he hit grade prep age right through to age 18. And I also wanted him to continue the mainstreaming because he was learning so many additional things.

When the time came to look at the list of kids who were coming through to the 4-year-old kinder program, Kaye studied the list to work out what we could do, and she noticed there were three other special needs children attending who were going to have aides in the room.

That meant we would have Kaye and her assistant Debbie, plus there would be a volunteer in the room every session, and there were two or three aides for the other special needs kids. There would also be parent helpers every session and if need be, I was happy to be there every session just so he could go.

Because of all the people who were going to be at each session, Kaye suggested we just enrol Darcy as a mainstream child without any special needs. So, we took the plunge, filled out the enrolment forms and waited to see if he would be accepted.

New Normal

I told the SDS principal what we were doing and assured him we would not be applying for any additional funding. The only funding that was going to be applied for was with the school. I explained to him about the extra children who would be at mainstream kinder with assistants and we were enrolling him as a mainstream child. He was worried that it wouldn't work out but wished us luck and hoped it would.

He got his enrolment through and we got through the whole year without attracting any questions. With the extra volunteers and staff in the room, we managed to get him everything he needed. I didn't have to be there every session, but I made sure I did parent help every couple of weeks.

During this time, he was doing two days mainstream, three days special. As the year went on, I stopped doing too many days at the kinder because Darcy seemed to achieve more without me there. When I was there, he expected me to do things for him. I didn't help at SDS and he needed to get used to me not being there. Darcy got to do everything that his older brothers did at kinder. He did the Christmas concert (he and Caleb had the same part – the little drummer boy), and graduated at the same preschool as his brothers. It's very special having the same special memories.

The year at 4-year-old kinder was huge. He achieved so many different things and the support we had was awesome. This was the year he ditched his walker and started walking on his own. What a celebration and victory that was. You could see how happy he was to achieve this. He could now do everything the other kids did, with practice. He could climb now because he didn't have to hang onto the walker. It was the best milestone!

The Unexpected Journey

The following year, Darcy started attending Langwarrin Park Primary School one day a week. This was the school his brothers went to and for us it was important for him to give this a try. When I was pregnant, I talked to the school principal at the time, Ray Flanagan about Darcy and what lay ahead for him with schooling. I remember mentioning to him that I was interested in dual schooling. He was so supportive and told me we would make sure we at least gave it a try.

Ted, Darcy's paediatrician, thought it was a great idea to start some dual schooling and see where it would take him. He explained to me things usually start to change when kids hit the Grade 3 mark, and the acceptance of the kids isn't there as much anymore. I remember thinking to myself I would be so happy if he made it to Grade 3. Darcy was verbal at this stage, but most people couldn't understand him, and I wasn't sure how long this development would take so I figured even a few years at Langwarrin Park would be fantastic. Mind you, the kids he was at school with knew exactly what he was saying and what he wanted. Kids are amazing.

I wanted him to experience the same things his brothers did during primary school, and the kids he went to kinder with were amazing. They were so understanding with Darcy. They had no problems helping him and they accepted him for who he was. They didn't worry about or see his disability.

With kinder graduation done and the school holidays over, it was time for his first official day at Langwarrin Park Primary School. He'd done really well with his transition days and he had no problem going off on the first day. I was so proud of him as I watched him go into his room with all of his friends. He waved goodbye to me with so much confidence.

Primary school was one day a week at Langwarrin and four days at SDS. We were extremely lucky and had an aide allocated to be with him for the whole day. We had met this woman before and knew she was very passionate about what she did. We were more than happy she was going to do this journey with Darcy. Her name is Trudi and she is an absolute angel. She has so much passion in her role with special needs children and children who just need some extra help. Over the years she would prove to be the best advocate for him at school and she was the driving force for making sure he got to have a go at everything.

She did so much to make sure that he got everything he needed at the school. He was included in absolutely everything. She helped the kids understand his disability and that he could participate in games and things like that just like they could, but he might need a little bit of extra help. She explained to them that if they helped him out, he would, in time, be able to do it.

We made the decision that we wanted him to participate in all the excursions and extracurricular activities, or as many as possible. We spoke to the principals and asked if we could have extra days sometimes or if we could swap days. Maybe if we had two days one week, we would have none the week after or we could work something out. Sometimes we ended up having extra days and sometimes we did whatever suited everyone else.

We were so happy because he was going to experience all the special things his brothers did. This was so special for Caleb and Blake because they could talk to him about the times they went on the same excursions or dressed up similar to him on the dress-up days. They loved being able to relive their special days at the school with him.

The Unexpected Journey

Throughout Darcy's school life, I did the same thing with the parents at the beginning of every year as I had done at the kinder. I wrote a letter at the beginning of the year so that the kids could be spoken to at home by their parents and told about Darcy and that they could ask any questions they wanted to. Some of the kids had already been with Darcy for two years at kinder, but there were also some new kids who hadn't met him before. It also opened that door for the parents to ask questions without feeling like they were asking the wrong thing or upsetting me. We had many days of conversation before and after school because of the letter I had given them.

As a parent of a special needs child, you would rather people ask questions than stare, make assumptions and gossip. Watching people stare at your child with confused looks on their faces or pointing is one of the hardest things you have to deal with as a parent of a child with special needs. Just come and ask a question if you have one or just say hello. Most questions people ask are very easy to answer and everyone goes away without feeling awkward or upset.

Langwarrin Park Primary School was such a great experience for Darcy and the kids he went through it with were some of the most amazing kids I've ever come across. They were so supportive of Darcy and looked forward to the day he was going to be there with them. Many of them called it Darcy Day. They were more than happy to help him with anything and never once teased him or thought it was too much trouble. Even when he did something he wasn't supposed to, Trudi taught them that they could tell him no otherwise he would never learn.

As the years went on, Darcy gained more and more confidence at Langwarrin Park Primary School. He was learning many different things from what he learned at SDS. He was learning different games in the playground and many things in the classroom as well. His teachers each year at SDS said it was a great thing for Darcy to be doing and they could see the value he got from it.

Over the years, Darcy attended excursions and participated in athletic days, swimming carnivals and even got to go on camps. Trudi went on the excursions and the specialist days with him. We decided it would be better for me not to go (especially in the early years) as he would play up for me. If he decided he didn't want to walk anymore, he would drop to the ground with me. With Trudi he would keep going with small rest breaks. It was amazing the things she could get him to do compared to what he would do for me.

Swimming and athletics carnivals were awesome. Darcy was nowhere near at the same level as his peers but that didn't matter. Their encouragement and cheering and sometimes even running or swimming at his pace, gave him the motivation to finish. They were amazing days to be a part of. Kids of such young ages knowing what was needed to help their classmate and not even thinking twice about it.

Grade 3 was the first camp Darcy went on. It was for two nights and three days and Trudi would go with him. We didn't need to worry about how he would sleep because he had always been a great sleeper and happy to go to bed when told. Trudi spent a lot of time with him and knew what he was capable of and what she could try with him. We didn't think it was going to be a problem and I filled out the forms and paid for the camp.

As it got closer however, some of the teachers were worried about how he would go. They had conversations with Trudi, and I had meetings with them as well. I answered all their questions and told them I wouldn't even consider sending him to camp if I didn't think he was going to cope. After a couple of meetings, we agreed that he would go, and they would see how he went on the first night. If he didn't cope, I would pick him up the next day, otherwise he would stay for the remainder of the camp.

The first day and night came and went, and he did really well. He participated in everything, even ate all the food and slept really well. Trudi kept me updated on how well everything was going and that he was having a ball. She said it had been great for the teachers to see him trying, succeeding and enjoying. I'll never forget picking him up from the bus and the teachers coming out one by one telling me, "Wow, what an amazing young boy you've got there." He just killed it. He smashed it. I was so very proud, and the tears were welling up. I was so happy to see him, and it was wonderful hearing about all of his adventures.

We have Trudi to thank for that because she really pushed and helped him feel comfortable to try things. She pushed at the school, reassuring them he would be fine. She even managed to get him on the giant swing. She said that took quite a while but once she got him onto it, he didn't want to get off. She took a video for us showing all the kids cheering for him. He was so proud of himself. There were very special moments right there. Inclusion at its absolute finest.

Grade 4, 5 and 6 camps were easier to get him to but there were always a few people who were worried about him going and what was going to happen. The kids were always so happy that he was going with them. We got through them the same as the Grade 3 camp and every time they returned, the teachers all said the same thing, that he was a delight to have and he was amazing in everything he accomplished.

New Normal

As I said earlier, we were so lucky the year that he started the kinder and the progression through to school with the kids he went with. They were fantastic and took it on board to include him in everything. In the early days they'd probably mothered him a bit, which was fine, and he soaked up every bit of it. But then as he got older Trudi taught them that they didn't have to mother him, and they would be better teaching him. She told them he just wanted to be with them, doing the same things.

His favourite game at mainstream school was four square. When he first started playing, he couldn't even hit the ball and would jump in whenever he wanted. By the end of grade six, he knew exactly what was going on. He knew he had to wait his turn and only jump in when someone went out. The kids learned that all this stuff could be taught, and Darcy could participate in anything.

Darcy went from Grade Prep right through to Grade 6. The years had gone by very quickly and we were so proud of him. His paediatrician was delighted as well. He didn't think he would get to Grade 6 even only doing one day a week. He thought the inclusion would stop at around Grade 3. He was very proud and happy for Darcy.

Darcy was my last child at primary school, and we enjoyed it so much. We didn't want it to end. Those seven years went so fast.

As in all the other years, he participated in everything in Grade 6. He went on camp, excursions and specialty days and was in the school production. Even though he wasn't there for all the rehearsals, they made sure he participated.

The school production was a really proud moment for us and him. He was more than happy to be a part of it (he loves the stage). One of the most special moments was his classmates from SDS coming to the school and watching him on stage. They got to meet his classmates from Langwarrin, and we got a photo of Darcy with both of his grades. I think it's my favourite photo from all the years he was at Langwarrin.

The graduation process at Langwarrin was great as he was a part of all of it. He went to Langwarrin three days that week so he could go on a special day out to the movies and lunch. One of the days they spent getting their special school days scrapbooks signed by friends and teachers. And on graduation night, watching him walk across the stage by himself, was one of the best moments ever. He seemed to get the biggest clap out of everybody…it was extremely emotional. I don't think it was just my emotions either. There weren't too many dry eyes in the house.

Initially, some of the teachers organising graduation planned for Trudi to walk across the stage with him. She didn't want to do that. She said she'd assisted him in his learning and accomplishments, but he did it all by himself and she thought he could walk across the stage to receive his certificate by himself. They had practiced and he wasn't the first one to go across, so he got to see his friends and what they did. I think there was some worry about what he would do on the stage, but they needn't have worried, he did it perfectly.

The children all had something said about them as they walked across the stage. Trudi helped Darcy with his, and his introduction went like this….

"Darcy loves to dance and loves to play four square with his friends. He has loved his time at Langwarrin Park and wants to thank everyone for their time and patience in making it such a special time."

Having him in mainstream schooling helped him and also helped the other children, teachers and parents. It taught acceptance and inclusion. It helped a lot of kids see that he was just like them in lots of ways, even though he was a little different in other ways. I always told the kids if they thought about it, we are all different. We are all good at some things and not at others. We all progress to things at our own pace, whether it's learning in the classroom or learning games. They all embraced that. The very last thing that we did at that school was his grade all forming a circle and singing the school song. They all made sure Darcy was in the circle before they started singing. That single moment was one of the times I realised that we had done the right thing. I think it helped with his physical development and his learning. I think it helped with his speech. I think it helped with lots of things.

The kids at Langwarrin Park probably don't realise it yet but the mateship, strength and inclusion they showed Darcy was second-to-none. I hope they realise one day how special these days were. They taught Darcy a lot of things and I hope one day they'll realise that. To be patient and not see his disability. They embraced Darcy for who "he" was and focused on what he could do and not what he couldn't.

Many of the teachers gained knowledge from Darcy attending the school, which was helped by Trudi being his assistant. There was nothing he didn't try and nothing he didn't succeed at. She came up with strategies and different ways he could achieve things and he nailed it every time. If it weren't for Trudi, I don't think we would have made it from Prep to Grade 6. She fought hard for him and gave me the strength to fight harder even when I thought it was no use. She was the best advocate for him at that school and we will forever love her.

She is now part of our family and we wouldn't have it any other way. The friendship we have with her is a very special one.

The Unexpected Journey

Acceptance and inclusion were number one at Langwarrin Park Primary School, and we smashed it. It was awesome. We have wonderful memories of them all.

Never stop fighting for your child and what you think is best for them. Whether they have a disability or not. We, as parents, know what our children can accomplish, and we should never lose sight of that and never stop trying.

The Unexpected Journey

CHAPTER 11
LIFE 2.0

Today, Darcy is 13 years old. He has finished his dual schooling and now attends Frankston SDS full-time.

The things that he learned at mainstream school have helped him at SDS and the teachers have told me they can see all the wonderful things he achieved there.

He is a very busy boy with out-of-school activities. He does dance with BAM Arts Inc, Special Olympics basketball, swimming, and Auskick. Over the years, with persistence, his skills have improved dramatically. Again, the people around him, coaches and other parents, have helped with spending a bit of extra time with him so he can reach his full potential.

We have some great things in place for him with our support worker Caroline. She helps with community access, taking him out and about without us. It's important for him to do things without us as he relies on us a lot without us even realising. With someone else he is a little more independent. He doesn't get to go out with a lot of his friends and their families, so Caroline taking him out replaces that. His brothers would go out with friends without us being there, and support workers allow that to happen more.

Caroline, our support worker, is fantastic. We couldn't have asked for anyone better. She really enjoys teaching him new skills and helping him. She is an extra hand to teach him self-care at home and he is much more willing to do it with her than with us. Where he will argue with us over doing something for quite a while, with Caroline he seems to do it straight away. Their relationship didn't take long to blossom into what it is now, which showed us she was the right choice. She has also become part of our family now and we love her dearly.

He also attended community days out and camps with Ozchild. Again, strengthening that independence without having us by his side. The camps were brilliant and allowed him to make different friends away from school.

He also does cooking with a company called 100 Mile Foodie. Jane Nimmo comes into the home and continues the independent living skills of cooking he learns at school.

I was finding that even though he was doing these skills at school he wasn't wanting to do them at home and wasn't willing to try different foods at home. At school, he eats what he cooks, or at least tries it. If I asked him to come and help me make a cake, he wouldn't and there was no budging him. When I found out about this program through a friend, I thought it sounded great, so I jumped on it straight away.

Life 2.0

It took a few weeks to get used to it being something he now does after school every week and he is starting to really look forward to it. He has very quickly learned to crack an egg, use knife cutting skills, make dough, and many other skills. It also helps with other areas such as his speech and fine motor skills. His speech pathologist and OT are seeing improvements in areas that were not there before. It is a slow progression, but it is going well and he's learning beneficial independent living skills.

One of the other reasons I wanted him to start with 100 Mile Foodie was because he is quite a fussy eater. Part of the process of him cooking is that he has to at least try what he has made. His sensory issues would kick in with different foods and I wanted to try and get him to learn that other things are okay to eat. This has worked and most nights now he eats the meals we have cooked for dinner.

He also helps in compiling the list of ingredients and Jane takes him shopping to find and pay for the things he needs. These are more skills which have filtered out to when he comes shopping with me. He now helps to find things and wants to pay at the end.

We use a visual board to help him go through the steps so he can see what is required. He has to get through all the steps before he can finish and have his iPad. The last three steps are cooking the food, eating the food, and then he can get his iPad and relax.

We do regular speech pathology every fortnight with Elizabeth Barker. As ongoing support now, he is really kicking some goals. Until last year, the sessions were on and off again depending on when we could get funding for it. Now, with the NDIS, we have ongoing support with funds, and we can make sure his therapy is continuous. This makes a huge difference and we have been able to see the benefits very quickly.

His speech pathologist Elizabeth has noticed a huge improvement in him very quickly and the regular visits have helped with that. She is an amazing lady who has helped with much more than speech.

We also have ongoing OT every fortnight now. The gorgeous Kate Wormell from Sprout Therapy Services sees him at school every session. She is teaching him lots of fine motor skills, as well as strength and self-care. We have noticed a vast improvement here also, especially with his willingness to do things. You don't realise how hard it is to teach someone some of the skills when your other kids just start doing it at a certain age. When you have a child who will be able to do it when taught, some things like taking a t-shirt off, are quite difficult to teach. We just do these things and think it's an easy skill, but when you're trying to teach someone how to do it and have to physically show them, it is really difficult. Having that extra support and extra practice at school and at home is phenomenal.

As I mentioned, Darcy also now does Special Olympics basketball. He has always loved basketball and has watched his brothers all his life and always wanted to play just like them. It's one of his favourite activities. We've already had one tournament, which was interesting and inspirational to watch. It was a wonderful day. The support from all the team with each other and how caring they are is amazing. They want to do well and win but it's not the main focus. The main focus with most of the athletes is to enjoy what they're doing. None of them are upset when they have to sit on the bench. They actually seemed to enjoy the rest and giving their friends a go.

The all-abilities dance Darcy does, which was created by the lovely Lisa Murphy for her gorgeous son Buster is another terrific community of people. Lisa began the group when Buster wanted to dance, and she couldn't find a facility for him to do it. So, she started BAM Arts Inc.

Life 2.0

We started about five years ago and it has been wonderful to watch it grow and how each child and adult blossom every week.

We have a huge concert every year, held at our local art centre in Frankston. There is no pressure for the kids to be perfect on stage and individual expression is encouraged. Darcy loves to do whatever he wants up on stage, but he also knows what he is meant to be doing!

The BAM Community is another environment of people without any judgement. People are always there to help and be a support when things seem negative. We are all going through similar stories and watching our kids blossom, grow and learn new skills is wonderful.

During winter, Darcy also plays Auskick. He first started when he was five at SDS. The kids from SEDA used to come and help, with an AFL representative overlooking everything as well as the teacher. It didn't continue at the school, so I enrolled him in our local Auskick clinic. I was a little nervous initially because it's not a special needs clinic and there are hundreds of kids who participate. He has been doing that for about five years and with persistence, the last two years have shown his skills really well. He used to need encouragement through every step of the clinic but the last couple of years, he has just gone off and done what he needed to do. Next year, if he wants to play, I will look for an all abilities football team for him to play on.

The Disabled Surfers Association also provide a wonderful activity for people with special needs. We are linked up with the Mornington Peninsula branch of the group. The Disabled Surfers Association is an organisation of volunteers from all walks of life who provide a wonderful opportunity for people of all abilities, size and age to surf in the ocean.

We first learned about this organisation when Darcy was quite young, through friends that had participated in events at Pt Leo and Inverloch.

We had decided from the start that this was something we would like to try once Darcy became old enough. He's a very cautious child who doesn't like to try things if he thinks there may be some danger involved. So, we decided to wait until he was old enough to understand that it was going to be all right.

2018 was the year we decided to take Darcy to Pt Leo to participate in this surfing event.

We had no idea what awaited us at the beach and to what extent the volunteer base was.

To say we were delightfully overwhelmed would be an understatement. There are over 200 volunteers at this event to make sure everything runs smoothly, and every participant gets an opportunity to experience the surf.

There are volunteers at the registration desk where you can borrow wet suits and beach bikes (these are for people in wheelchairs so they can access the beach easily). There are volunteers at each station to make sure everyone has a fair chance. There are people cooking a BBQ to feed everyone, people distributing drinks of water, and a huge amount of people on the beach with the surfboards.

There are many experienced surfers who oversee everyone and help the new volunteers learn what is required to make sure participants are happy and safe on the boards.

Life 2.0

It is a day full of love, acceptance, inclusion and generosity. When you look around at the hundreds of people on the beach, there is nobody there without a smile on their face.

It is the most amazing day you will ever be a part of and is the most heart-warming experience.

We have taken Darcy to five events now at Pt Leo and Inverloch, and each time he gets a little more daring in how he sits on the surfboard. He seems to try something a little new each time we go.

The smile on his face and sense of achievement is one of the best things you will ever see. And the friends we have made are some of the most wonderful people you will ever meet. The events run during the warmer months – from January through to March - and every year we make sure they are marked on our calendar.

We have also been very fortunate to be involved with Variety – the Children's Charity Victoria who support kids and families who are facing many challenges through sickness, disadvantage or living with special needs. They help to allow kids to gain mobility, get out and about in the community, communicate, achieve independence and increase their self-esteem. They make sure the kids who miss out can always join in.

They allow parents to apply for grants for various things to help kids with independence and access to things they otherwise wouldn't be able to.

Our first grant with Variety was for Darcy to continue to attend mainstream school one day a week during his Grade 6 year. The money they granted us ensured Darcy was able to participate in all school activities in his last year of primary school including camp and all the graduation activities the other kids were going to be taking part in.

Our second grant was for a modified bike so that Darcy could learn and enjoy riding a bike that looked like everyone else's. The bike he previously had was a large 3-wheeler bike and because he was attending mainstream school, we thought it was important for him to ride a bike that looked like his friends' bikes.

The bike is a normal 2-wheeler bike with modified training wheels and modifications to the handlebars, brake and pedals. Darcy's OT also recommended this bike as the modifications would allow Darcy to learn how to ride and eventually lose the training wheels.

The bike came from Solve Disability Solutions and was modified exactly to what Darcy needed. After an initial fitting, once the grant was released it was ready to pick up. Darcy feels very safe and comfortable on the bike and we can see that it won't be too long before he is riding without the training wheels.

Through Variety we were also given an opportunity to be part of the AFLX preseason competition this year. Patrick Dangerfield chose Variety as his charity of choice and Darcy was lucky enough to be picked to represent them.

We went to Marvel stadium where Darcy and four other children from various charities had to choose a ball with a number on it. This number was the order in which the captains chose their teams.

This selection process was aired on television which was not only exciting for us all to see Darcy, but also showed people the charities that were involved.

Life 2.0

The kids all got to keep the balls and had their captains sign them. We met all of the players and also had a chance to go to the AFLX games on the night they played.

Variety also hosts a wonderful Christmas Party every year at the Melbourne Exhibition Centre. Everything provided for the kids is donated and everyone working are volunteers. It's an amazing day allowing the kids to try rides and participate in lots of different activities as well as meet lots of wonderful characters including Santa (the favourite with Darcy).

It is wonderful being part of the Variety family. Not only do they provide grants, but they also are very supportive and helpful.

Darcy's brothers are still great with him. They are now 21 and 18 and have very different relationships with him. Caleb seems to have a very nurturing relationship with him and tells him when he is doing the wrong thing. They play and stir each other up a bit too. Their favourite game to play is with Nerf guns. It gets very chaotic but is so great to watch.

Blake also has a very nurturing relationship with him, but he and Darcy like to annoy each other. Their favourite game with each other is basketball. He got a basketball ring for his birthday so when the weather is good, out they go. Darcy likes to hide Blake's things, but it is usually always something Blake needs the next day and Darcy just sits there with a grin not telling where he has hidden it.

Our gorgeous Bree has a lovely bond with Darcy too, even though they don't see each other much. She's our little travelling gypsy, but we keep her updated with photos and videos.

The Unexpected Journey

Mick and I do what we can for him and try to make sure he has every opportunity to learn and thrive. We love to take Darcy out to lots of different events. We have been to concerts and theatre as well as many other things. His favourite, I think, was seeing Pink live. I found myself watching him more than the concert and so did a few people around us. At the end of the concert they commented on how wonderful it was to watch him enjoy it so much.

We love him dearly, we love all our boys dearly, and we do whatever we can for all three of them, whatever they need.

Darcy can be quite bossy at times and tries very hard not to do things. He likes to be waited on hand and foot…who wouldn't. He has us both wrapped around his little finger but has us both conned in different areas. When I am home, he likes to get me to get his food and other things, and sometimes, without thinking, I just do it. I have to remind myself he is 13 and can do most things on his own now.

When I am at work at night, he always cons Mick into letting him stay up until I get home. When I walk in the door, I will ask why he is still up. He just starts to giggle, and Mick will always say he was missing me. Needless to say, he gets straight to bed when I get home.

I think we are a pretty cool family, and I think Darcy is growing up quite well and slowly learning to become more independent. He still needs assistance with things, but he gets to do everything that the older boys did when they were young. He gets to do everything any other child would do. He loves going to the movies, going to friend's houses, bowling, the park and heaps of other things.

One of our friends has had him for sleepovers and we have had her son once now too. That has been really good, because it doesn't happen a lot in the disability world. Because of different complications with certain disabilities, I think it is just easier to have a playdate instead. His gorgeous friend Evan and his family have been so great having Darcy stay over. He and Evan have developed a beautiful friendship over the years and the sleepovers are something they both look forward to.

Darcy is an amazing young man who is very social. He loves to go out with his family, and his friends. When dinner is ready, he calls everybody to the dinner table and doesn't stop until everyone is out with their plates. He has been doing this even before he was eating the food I was cooking, which is quite funny.

I have written my book because I want people to give everyone a chance. Don't label people and put them in a box because, if you give them a chance, they might just surprise you. We're all human beings and we've all got the same feelings and emotions. I constantly wonder if what I'm doing for him is right, but it's no different to how I felt with my other boys. I'm always wondering if I'm doing the right thing. I think that just comes with being a mum. All our kids are different, and all need different types of care. They all reach milestones at different times and they all need extra training in certain things. Special needs children need more, some more than others, but as a mum I do this stuff without even thinking about it. I love helping Darcy, but I also love when he achieves new things. I often have to tell myself to teach and let him accomplish instead of doing it for him, but sometimes that doesn't work, sometimes it just happens.

Our unexpected journey, even though unexpected initially, has been and still is one of the most wonderful rides of our life. The people we have met along the way are some of the best people we have ever met.

The Unexpected Journey

The friends that have been in our lives for a long time, like my friends Liz and Julie and many of our other friends, have accepted Darcy for who he is right from the start. Their support has helped immensely, and we are so very lucky to have them in our lives.

I talk a lot about us helping Darcy and getting things to assist him with his goals, but he has definitely (and is still) teaching us lessons every day.

One of my friends once told me she was sure Darcy chose us as his family so he could teach the people of our community acceptance. I remember thinking at the time she was just saying that to help with my doubts, but she was right. The amount of people he has already had effects on is amazing.

People I don't even really know often ask how he is and want to know what he is up to. I have lots of social media requests from people just wanting to keep up with how Darcy is going.

Disability is a scary world to enter but it is one of the best worlds we have come into.

We look forward to what wonderful things lie ahead for us as a family.

Life 2.0

Life 2.0

CHAPTER 12
ACCEPTANCE/ INCLUSION

All we ever want for our children is for them to be accepted and included among their peers, and in the community we live in.

We want them to learn and enjoy life and not have to worry about what other people are thinking.

Unfortunately, there is a lot of judgement in the world and not enough inclusion or acceptance.

With social media, we are able to see a whole range of different people and their accomplishments which gives us hope for our children and what the future may hold. I hope that because of this, people will open their minds more to children and adults with disabilities and see what they can achieve and that they want to enjoy life like everyone else.

The Unexpected Journey

Darcy was thrust into a life that was very busy and around a lot of people. I was coordinating the local Auskick clinic, coaching and team-managing the older boys' basketball teams, and helping at their primary school almost every day.

He was put in front of people from the moment he was born. Most people were very accepting and full of questions. I didn't know all the answers and still probably don't. Things change with him, as they do with all of us, every day.

Questions are great if you are curious about something or someone. Most of the people I know with children with disabilities would prefer people to come and say hi and ask questions if they are wondering about something. It's much better than staring or pointing.

Children are children no matter how different you may think they are. They want the same thing as any other child…to be loved, to have friends, to learn and to join in with play and other things kids do. Children with disabilities may not be able to do the same things as others physically, but they like to be part of things.

None of us are the same, yet if we appear 'normal' to people, we are accepted and included. When some people see a disability, they put up a wall.

I want people to know that everyone deserves a chance. Everyone deserves to be looked at for who they are and not what they have. If they open up their mind and heart, they will probably be surprised at the beauty they find.

Darcy is a boy who loves people. He has a lot to give and a lot to teach. We may not know he is teaching us until we have thought about it later, but he teaches us every day.

Acceptance/Inclusion

He has a wonderful sense of compassion and when people are feeling down, he immediately goes to them to make sure they are all right. He doesn't like it when people are upset or sad and tries to help.

A great example is from a few years ago. A friend of mine Sharon had lost her son and I hadn't seen her since it had happened. We bumped into each other at our local shopping centre and started talking about what had happened and how she was going. Darcy was playing near us while we spoke and then Sharon said hello to him. He was only about five at the time and when she spoke to him, he looked at her, walked over and embraced her. It was a hug he knew she needed. He held onto her until he felt the hug had done its job. The two of us were very emotional, but she said he was amazing and knew she needed that. It was a beautiful moment.

Darcy loves to do activities like other kids do like football, basketball, singing, dancing and playing with his friends. He is a very funny boy and loves to make people laugh. Sometimes he doesn't have an off switch, but I don't think that's so bad. He loves to perform and put on a show for his friends and family.

We made a choice 13 years ago to bring a little boy with Down Syndrome into our family and we don't regret that choice ever. In a strange way, I think he helped us to make that choice because he needed to be here.

He teaches us lessons every day and most certainly brings light into our home. He is an amazing little boy and we wouldn't have him any other way.

At 13 he knows when people are mocking him or staring, and he doesn't understand or like it. To him, everyone is the same.

The Unexpected Journey

So next time you see someone with a disability, give them a chance to shine. Even if it's just a smile you give them. That small gesture is a huge step towards acceptance and inclusion.

Remember to always look at the person and not the disability. The disability does not define them, it is just a part of them.

ABOUT THE AUTHOR

Julie Fisher was born in Carlton, Melbourne and raised by Werner and Irene Pallmann. Her childhood and early teen years were spent in Albury until she was 4, Elwood until she was 9, Caulfield North until she was 12 and the rest of her teenage years in Bentleigh.

She finished school in Year 11 at McKinnon Secondary College and did a year at Moorabbin TAFE where she obtained a secretarial certificate.

She worked in accounting for 18 years followed by one year at a temp agency, predominantly working in an outpatients psychiatric centre. She has now been a gaming attendant at Berettas Langwarrin Hotel for almost 10 years.

She is wife to Mick, mum to Caleb, Blake and Darcy, and step-mum to Bree.

She has always had a passion for writing and enjoyed writing essays and short stories in high school and after she had graduated.

The Unexpected Journey

She has had a burning passion and dream to write a book since she was in school but never thought the dream would ever become a reality until now.

In 2018 she met Stuart and Natasa Denman and began the journey to fulfilling her dream with Ultimate 48 Hour Author.

After many months and many moments of self-doubt, her dream has become a reality and she has given life to her dream of a book in The Unexpected Journey. She hopes that this book will show people the beautiful side of disability and raise awareness for inclusion and acceptance.

Julie has done public speaking in her roles at her children's school, as team manager for her sons' basketball teams and in her role as coordinator of a local Auskick centre. She looks forward to many more public speaking events with the release of her book.

She has enjoyed this journey of bringing her dream to reality and after finishing this book, she has the drive to now complete another book. Watch this space for the next story.

"When you feel like giving up on your dream, force yourself to work another day, another week, another year.

You'll be amazed what happens when you don't give up."

Nick Vujicic

LINKS FOR SUPPORT GROUPS, THERAPY SERVICES AND GROUPS:

Down Syndrome Victoria – www.downsyndromevictoria.org.au

Monash Children's Hospital – www.monashchildrenshospital.org

Association for Children with a Disability – www.acd.org.au

Carers Victoria – www.carersvictoria.org.au

Sprout Paediatric Services – www.sprouttherapyservices.com.au

NDIS – www.ndis.gov.au

BAM Arts Inc. – www.bamallstars.org.au

Special Olympics Victoria – www.specialolympics.com.au/vic

100 Mile Foodie – www.100milefoodie.com.au

Variety – The Children's Charity Victoria – www.variety.org.au/VIC

Disabled Surfers Association – www.disabledsurfers.org

For updates to list of organisations, bookmark my webpage www.juliefisher.com.au

THE UNEXPECTED JOURNEY

ENGAGE JULIE FISHER AS YOUR NEXT SPEAKER

Julie Fisher's Unexpected Journey began just before the birth of her third son.

After making a decision to provide a life of love, experiences and positivity, Julie shares her family's journey in a raw and real way, engaging the audience with her honesty and insights into the world of disability.

Julie is available to speak to support groups, organisations and schools on:

Finding the Joy in Disability

Creating the Experiences and Life that Everyone Deserves

The Special Family Connections that Enrich our Lives

Contact Julie at juliedixie@hotmail.com to enquire about her speaking at your event, availability and rates.

Julie will often speak at non-for-profits free of charge.

The Unexpected Journey

Having a child with Down Syndrome is like taking the scenic route

**You still get where you are going
It may take a little longer
But it will be well worth the trip!**

Author Unknown

www.ingramcontent.com/pod-product-compliance
Lightning Source LLC
Chambersburg PA
CBHW031118080526
44587CB00011B/1019